New York

NEW YORK BY ROAD

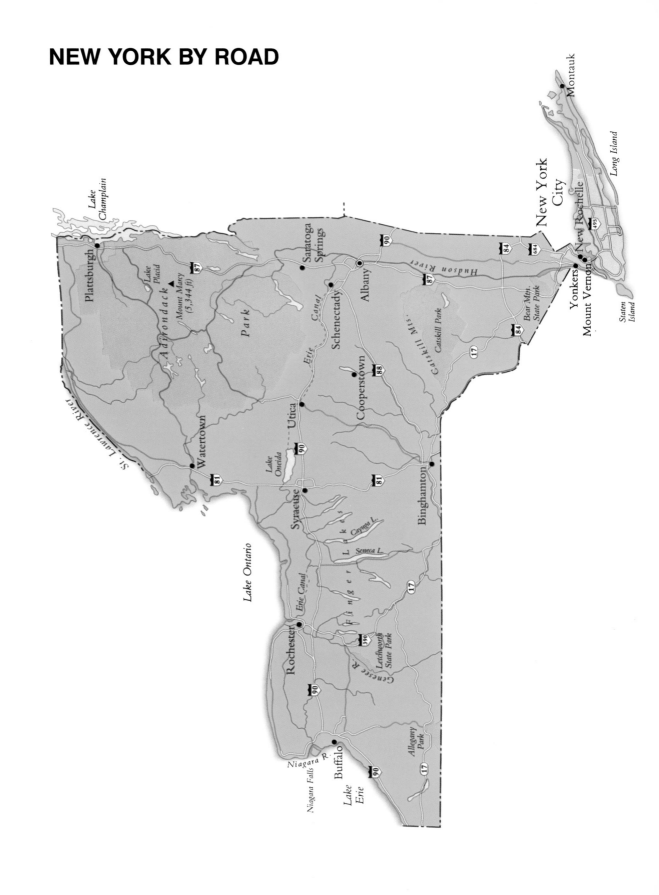

Celebrate the States

New York

Virginia Schomp

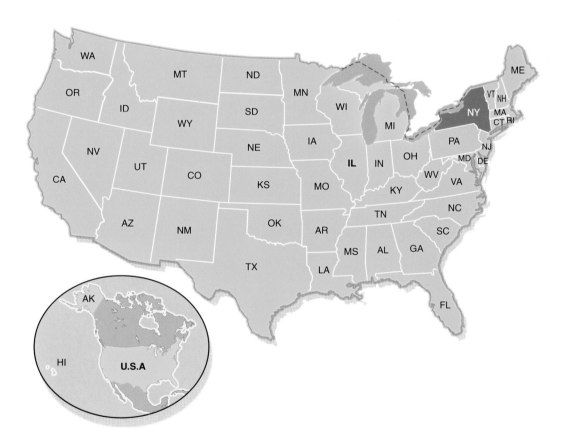

mc Marshall Cavendish
Benchmark
New York

To Chip,
who has moved from elementary school to college between editions
and still makes being a mom the best job in any state

Marshall Cavendish Benchmark
99 White Plains Road
Tarrytown, New York 10591-9001
www.marshallcavendish.us

All Internet sites were correct and accurate when sent to press.

Library of Congress Cataloging-in-Publication Data

Schomp, Virginia.
New York / by Virginia Schomp.— 2nd ed.
p. cm. — (Celebrate the states)
Includes bibliographical references and index.
ISBN 0-7614-1738-9
1. New York (State)—Juvenile literature. I. Title. II. Series.
F119.3.S36 2005   974.7'044—dc22   2004000853

Series redesign by Adam Mietlowski

Photo research by Candlepants Incorporated

Cover photo: Scott Barrow, Inc. /Super Stock

The photographs in this book are used by permission and through the courtesy of: *Index Stock:* Paul Katz, 8; Henryk T. Kaiser, 10, 106; David Urbina, 81. *Super Stock:* Super Stock Inc., 12; Arienne Sandler, 54; Kevin Moan, 107. *Getty Images:* Anne Ackermann, 13, 46; Peter Gridley, 17; Michael Melford, back cover. *The Image Works:* Dennis Nett/Syracuse Newspapers, 16; Syracuse Newspapers, 18; David M. Jennings, 20; Mike Roy/Syracuse Newspaper, 22; Bob Mahoney, 23, 101; Monika Graff, 45, 84, 94; Ethel Wolvovitz, 48; Richard Lord, 52; David M. Grossmann, 55; Rommel Pecson, 62; Jeff Greenberg, 63, Steve Ruark/Syracuse Newspapers, 64; Howard Drach, 73; Mitch Wojnarowicz/Amsterdam Recorder, 82; Kathy McLaughlin, 87, 89; Visual & Written/Nano Calvo, 112. *Bridgeman Art Library:* Hudson Bay Company, Canada, 24; Chicago Historical Society, Chicago,USA, 32; Bibliotheque Nationale, Paris, France, Archives Charmet; 33. *Art Resource, NY:* Smithsonian American Art Museum, Washington DC, 26; Snark, 39; The New York Public Library, 41. *Corbis:* 70; Bettmann, 29, 30, 38, 42, 43, 128, 129; SYGMA/Schwarz Shaul, 51; Girl Ray, 58; Ramin Talaie, Seth Wenig/Stringer/Reuters, 60; Larry Lee Photography, 68; James Leynse, 77; Raymond Gehman, 85; John Madere, 93; Mark E. Gibson, 97; Lester Lefkowitz, 98, 110; Lee Snider/Photo Images, 102; Joseph Sohm, ChromoSohm Inc. 104; dbox for the Lower Manhattan Development Corporation, 111; Clayton J. Price, 113; William Manning, 118; Chris Jones, 122; Leif Skoogfors, 123; Francis G. Mayer, 124; SYGMA/Markowitz Jeffrey, 126; Matthew Mendelsohm, 130; Szenes Jasons, 131. *Photo Researchers Inc.:* Millard H. Sharp, 115(top); John Kaprelian, 115 (low).

Printed in China

1 3 5 6 4 2

Contents

New York is people . . .

"Here individuals of all nations are melted into a new race of men."

— French settler St. Jean de Crèvecoeur

"Being a New Yorker is as much a condition as it is a geographic description of where you choose to live. Millions of us are people who have come here from all over the world . . . because they believe that . . . if they work hard here, they can rise above what they were when they were born."

— journalist David Halberstam

. . . and unforgettable places.

"I find in . . . New York . . . the best and most effective medicine my soul has yet partaken—the grandest physical habitat and surroundings of land and water the globe affords."

— poet Walt Whitman

"No matter how you look at New York City—vertically, horizontally, upside down, sideways—one thing remains clear. New York City is the Capital of the World."

— former New York mayor Rudolph Giuliani

No state has a richer history.

"The land of Ganono-o or 'Empire State' as you love to call it, was once laced by our trails from Albany to Buffalo . . . trails worn so deep by the feet of the Iroquois that they became your own roads of travel."

— a Cayuga chief

"To Europe she was America, to America she was the gateway of the earth. But to tell the story of New York would be to write a social history of the world."

— writer H. G. Wells

No state has been so loved . . .

"The biggest bridges and the deepest tunnels and the greatest water works and the best damn parks. You name it, we did it."
—former U.S. senator Daniel Patrick Moynihan

"The true New Yorker secretly believes that people living anywhere else have to be, in some sense, kidding."
—writer John Updike

. . . so unappreciated . . .

"I don't like the life here. There is no greenery. It would make a stone sick."
—former Soviet premier Nikita Khruschev, visiting New York City

. . . or so greatly challenged.

"September 11, 8:46 a.m. . . . at that hour we saw the worst of mankind. We saw the face of evil. . . . We also saw the best of humanity, the best of New York, in our response."
—New York governor George Pataki

Most of all, New York is a state of contrasts. It is towering cities and noisy factories. It is quiet villages, rolling farmland, and unspoiled wilderness. New York is millions of people from a hodgepodge of cultures all laughing and debating in a never-ending symphony of voices. There's no other place like it. With all its contrasting treasures, New York is a state bursting with energy and full of surprises.

Chapter One

Gateway to America

When you think of New York, you might picture soaring skyscrapers and city streets bustling with activity. But New York is much more than its most famous city. It is a varied and spectacular landscape of mountains, lakes, rivers, forests, and ocean beaches. It is millions of people at work and play in vibrant cities, thriving suburbs, and quiet country towns. At the same time, New York is home to an abundant array of wildlife, from woodchucks and deer to black bears and majestic bald eagles.

MAGICAL LANDSCAPES

In ancient times New York was one vast plain, with a line of tall mountains in the north. Then, more than a million years ago, colossal glaciers ground their way across the landscape. They rounded the mountaintops, carved out lakes and valleys, and dumped huge deposits of dirt. By the time the ice melted, New York had been transformed. Its new landscape included four different types of landforms: upland, plateau, lowland, and coastal plain.

New Yorkers relax among the trees and meadows of Central Park, in the heart of New York City.

The rugged Adirondack region is the country's largest wilderness area outside Alaska, with nearly two thousand mountains and three thousand lakes and ponds.

Upland

The east of New York has two mountainous regions, the Adirondack Upland and the New England Upland. The Adirondack Upland is a loose grouping of hills and mountains. These include Mount Marcy, New York's highest peak, at 5,344 feet. Thickly forested, the Adirondacks are wild and beautiful, with hundreds of lakes, streams, and waterfalls. The New England Upland includes the wooded Taconic Mountains and the low hills of Manhattan Island, the heart of New York City.

Plateau

Perched like a high table above the surrounding lowlands, the Appalachian Plateau in south-central New York is the state's largest land region. Here the storybook character Rip Van Winkle slept among the "magical hues and shapes" of the Catskill Mountains.

The Tug Hill Plateau sits at the center of the state, east of Lake Ontario and west of the Adirondacks. Its varied landscape includes streams, rivers, wetlands, and large expanses of undeveloped forest.

Lowland

New York's low plains are home to the state's most fertile farmland. The Saint Lawrence Lowland is made up of a narrow corridor along the Saint Lawrence River, plus an area bordering Lake Champlain. The Great Lakes Lowland, which touches Lakes Erie and Ontario, is dotted with swamps and oval-shaped hills called drumlins. The Hudson-Mohawk Lowland is a narrow stretch of green valleys carved out by the Hudson and Mohawk rivers.

Coastal Plain

The low-lying Atlantic Coastal Plain takes in Long Island and three boroughs, or sections, of New York City: Queens, Brooklyn, and

A tall lighthouse stands guard on one of Long Island's sandy beaches.

Staten Island. Long Island starts near the lower edge of Manhattan and stretches 120 miles to the east. Its southern shore is fringed with sandy ocean beaches.

A WEALTH OF WATERS

The source of New York's most famous river, the Hudson, is a small lake named Tear of the Clouds, found high atop Mount Marcy, in the heart of the Adirondacks. From this high peak, the river flows more than three hundred miles south to the Atlantic Ocean. Near its mouth the Hudson rises and falls with the ocean tides. Native Americans called it Muhheakunnuk, or "the water that flows both ways."

Even longer than the Hudson is the Saint Lawrence River. This waterway on the New York–Canadian border flows out of Lake Ontario. A scattering of rocky islands called the Thousand Islands dots the blue waters where lake and river meet.

Farther west is one of the world's shortest rivers, the Niagara. Along its thirty-six-mile journey north from Lake Erie to Lake Ontario, this river takes a spectacular plunge down a rock ledge at Niagara Falls. French missionary Father Louis Hennepin was the first to write in awe of the "incredible Cataract or Waterfall, which has no equal."

New York is home to nearly eight thousand lakes. Many of these nestle among the foothills and mountains of the Adirondack region.

Three young women take a plunge into a clear blue lake nestled in the Adirondack Mountains.

Two of the Great Lakes, Erie and Ontario, share their shores with both New York and Canada. Lake Champlain sits on New York's border with Vermont. Oneida Lake, in central New York, is the largest lake completely within the state. To its west are the eleven Finger Lakes, long narrow strips of deep blue scooped out by the ancient glaciers.

CLIMATE CONTRASTS

Summer temperatures in New York City can climb to 95°F or higher. High humidity often makes it feel even hotter. "Working in the city in the summer—forget about it," says printing-press operator Kerry Martin. "The streets are like a steambath. If I didn't work in air-conditioning, I wouldn't survive."

Farther inland and in the mountains, summer is cooler. July averages a pleasant 66°F in the central Adirondacks.

Winter brings even greater contrasts. By the ocean, in Manhattan and Long Island, winter temperatures are relatively mild, generally hovering around the freezing mark, 32°F. The same is true beside Lakes Erie and Ontario. However, in these areas winter squalls can dump an incredible amount of "lake effect" snow. This type of snowfall occurs when cold arctic air moves over the warmer lake waters, causing moisture to evaporate rapidly into the air and form snow clouds. Great Lakes cities such as Rochester, Buffalo, and Syracuse are often buried under one winter storm after another.

The coldest parts of New York are the Saint Lawrence Valley and the upland and plateau regions. Winter temperatures in these parts of the state often drop below zero. Tug Hill Plateau is blanketed with more than two hundred inches of snow a year, making it the snow capital of the east.

LAND AND WATER

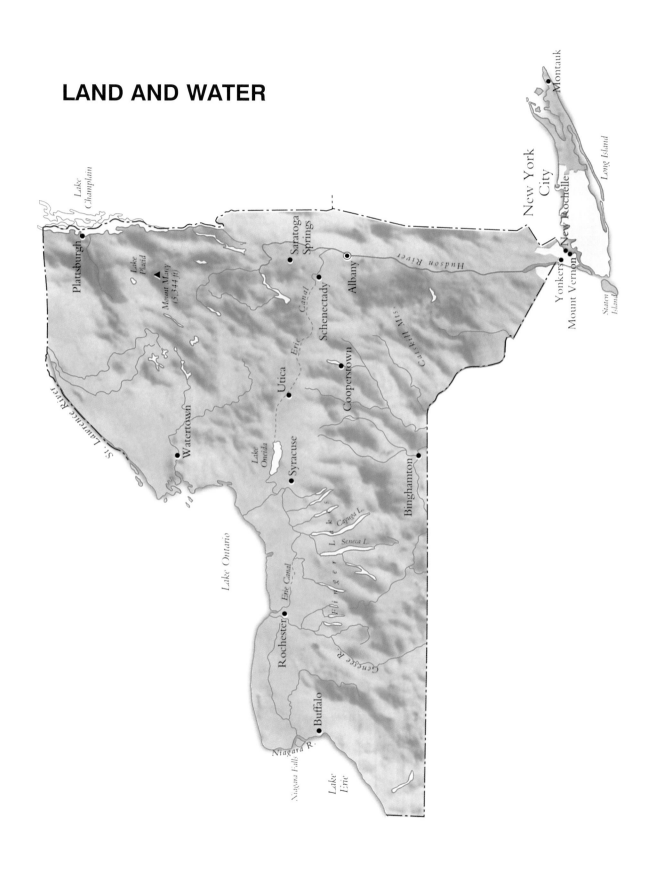

Montauk

Long Island

Lake
Champlain

New York
City

New Rochelle

Yonkers
Mount Vernon

Staten
Island

Plattsburgh

Lake
Placid

▲ Mount Marcy
(5,344 ft)

Saratoga
Springs

Albany

Hudson River

Schenectady

Catskill Mts

Erie Canal

Cooperstown

St. Lawrence River

Utica

Watertown

Lake
Oneida

Syracuse

Binghamton

Cayuga L.

Seneca L.

Lake Ontario

F i n g e r   L a k e s

Erie Canal

Rochester

Genesee R.

Buffalo

Niagara R.

Niagara Falls

Lake
Erie

New Yorkers take even the coldest, snowiest winters in stride. In fact, they often turn them into a celebration. Many cities and towns by the Great Lakes and in the Adirondacks salute snow season with winter carnivals. The fun includes snow sculpting, dogsled races, and sports such as broom hockey, snow softball, and volleyball on ice. The village of Saranac Lake, in the northern Adirondacks, is the frosty setting for the eastern United States' oldest winter festival. Activities center around a sparkling ice palace built from more than 1,500 huge blocks of ice cut from nearby Lake Flower.

A winter storm has turned this hill outside Syracuse into a playground for sledders.

PLANTS AND TREES

New York's great variety of landforms and habitats makes it a perfect home for many different types of animals and plants.

More than half of the state is covered in forests, with more than 150 types of trees. Evergreens found in New York include hemlocks, pines, and spruces. Among the many deciduous trees, which lose their leaves each autumn, are beeches, ashes, oaks, and maples. New York's state tree is the sugar maple. In the fall this tree's leaves change from green to brilliant shades of yellow, orange, and red. The sugar maple's wood is used in making furni-

Autumn brings spectacular colors to Taughannock Falls State Park in northern New York.

ture and other items. Its sweet sap is collected in late winter and early spring to make maple syrup.

In spring and summer, wildflowers paint New York in a rainbow of colors. Some of the state's most common wildflowers are the black-eyed Susan, daisy, violet, wild rose, goldenrod, buttercup, and the humble dandelion.

WILD THINGS

New York is home to 103 different types of mammals, more than any other northeastern state. Some of these animals thrive in a variety of habitats. Found throughout the state are the white-footed mouse, eastern chipmunk, gray squirrel, groundhog, raccoon, skunk, and white-tailed deer. Some live only in certain types of habitats. Beavers are found near ponds, rivers, and streams bordered with trees. Black bears live in or near large forests. The cool northern regions are home to cottontail rabbits, bobcats, coyotes, and moose. The ocean waters off Long Island help support more than thirty species of marine mammals. Among these are dolphins, seals, and the world's largest animal, the giant blue whale.

New York has more than three hundred types of birds, including both seasonal visitors and year-round residents. Spring and summer bring blackbirds, red-breasted robins, ruby-throated hummingbirds, and the clatter of

New York is home to more than a million white-tailed deer. Adult deer are usually reddish tan or gray, but a very few may be all-white, like this doe with its spotted fawn.

woodpeckers rapping on tree trunks and telephone poles. A familiar sign of autumn are the V-shaped flocks of Canada geese heading for winter nesting sites in New York. Hardy year-round residents include crows, pigeons, starlings, sparrows, and mourning doves. The state's best-known native bird is the bald eagle.

Many of New York's birds find their food in the state's lakes and rivers. These bodies of freshwater are home to hundreds of kinds of fish, including trout, salmon, bass, perch, pike, catfish, and spiny-finned sunfish. Bays and coastal waters teem with saltwater fish. Among these are bluefish, swordfish, and flat-bodied flounder, which change their color to match the sea bottom. The ocean waters off New York City and Long Island have rewarded fishermen with some amazing catches. The all-time record was set in 1986, when Don Braddick of Montauk reeled in a 3,450-pound great white shark.

ENVIRONMENTAL CHALLENGES

Ever since the first European settler's shack rose beside the Hudson River, New Yorkers have been building. Their busy hands have produced homes, offices, factories, highways, canals, bridges, and skyscrapers. Sadly, it seems that wherever people have built, environmental problems have followed.

New York's air, water, and land have been badly polluted. City dwellers breathe unhealthy fumes from cars, buses, trucks, power plants, factories, and other sources. Winds carry some of those pollutants across the state, and some fall to Earth in the form of acid rain. This extremely damaging form of pollution contaminates forests, lakes, and streams. The polluted waters in turn poison fish, birds, and other wildlife. A 2001 study found that one-quarter of the lakes in the Adirondacks were seriously acidic. Other studies have shown that people exposed to the effects of acid rain can suffer breathing problems and other illnesses.

New York's water quality has also suffered from more direct forms of pollution. For decades city sewers and factories pumped untreated waste into lakes and rivers. In both cities and rural areas, storm waters carried pollutants such as road salt and pesticides into the state's waters. In the 1970s many of New York's rivers and lakes were declared unsafe for swimming or fishing. The Mohawk River was covered with a sheen of oil and filth. Onondaga Lake in central New York was a cesspool, used mainly for the disposal of sewage and industrial wastes.

Garbage is another environmental problem. New Yorkers toss out nearly 23 million tons of trash each year, and the state is running out of places to put it. Most garbage is buried in smelly landfills. Rotting wastes can leak from older, unlined landfills, polluting underground water supplies.

As landfills have run out of room, New York has begun to ship garbage to other states. New York City alone sends out a nine-mile-long convoy of trucks each day, loaded with trash bound for sites up to three hundred miles away. Getting rid of all that garbage, said one city official, is "like a military-style operation on a daily basis."

An environmental engineer takes samples of water from the Hudson River to test for pollutants. In recent years New York has worked hard to reduce pollution in the state's rivers, lakes, and streams.

Even more worrisome are sites used as dumping grounds for hazardous wastes. In 2002 New York had more than 750 toxic-waste sites that had not yet been investigated or cleaned up, plus more than 10,000 "brownfields"—sites such as abandoned factories or gas stations that are considered less toxic but still dangerous.

The state's most infamous toxic dump is Love Canal, in the city of Niagara Falls. This neighborhood including homes and a school was built on top of land that had been used as a dumpsite for industrial chemicals. In the late 1970s, residents were evacuated after many began to get sick from the leaking wastes. Today a section of Love Canal remains surrounded by a fence, declared permanently off-limits.

CLEANING UP THE MESS

New York's environmental problems are serious. Fortunately, so are its plans for solving them. In fact, the state has some of the most aggressive environmental protection and conservation policies in the country.

In 1883 New York established the first state park, the Niagara Reservation State Park. Ten years later, it created the Adirondack Forest Preserve, adding a clause to the state constitution to ensure that millions of acres of undeveloped land would remain "forever wild." Over time a variety of government agencies and departments were established to protect the state's natural resources. Finally, in 1970, one "superagency" was established to unite all the groups and programs. The New York State Department of Environmental Conservation has broad responsibilities that include protecting the state's land, water, air, wildlife, and other natural resources and promoting public health and safety.

Since the late 1970s, state environmental programs have achieved significant success. Air quality has improved, and most rivers and lakes are again safe for swimming and fishing. Communities no longer pollute their waters with raw sewage. Hundreds of leaking landfills have been closed. Hundreds of other sites containing toxic wastes have been identified and scheduled for cleanup.

Much of the recent progress toward cleaner air and water has come through the Clean Water, Clean Air Bond Act. This $1.75 billion environmental cleanup and protection measure was proposed by Governor George Pataki in 1996. "We have been blessed with some of the world's greatest natural resources," said the governor. "This blessing carries with it the responsibility to care for these resources so

Environmental science students search for tiny lifeforms in dirt, moss, and other debris from a central New York lake.

they are there for our children." New Yorkers clearly agreed. Voters of different political parties united to pass the act by an impressive 56 percent.

As part of the Bond Act, New York's government has bought more than 30,000 acres of environmentally important land for protection. In many cases the state has worked out partnerships with businesses and citizens' groups to conserve resources while providing jobs and recreation. One example is Champion Lands. New York bought this vast stretch of forests, lakes, rivers, and wetlands in the northern Adirondacks from private owners in 1999. The purchase agreement preserved thousands of acres of undeveloped wilderness and sensitive wildlife habitat. It also opened up the land for hiking, hunting, camping, and other outdoor activities, as well as allowing for carefully managed logging. The land purchase, said one Department of Environmental Conservation official, opened "some of the most spectacular wild rivers in North America to the public for the first time in more than a century, while maintaining jobs vital to the North Country's economy."

While New York's environmental progress is encouraging, many challenges remain. The bottoms of many lakes and rivers remain polluted with toxins. Hundreds of toxic-waste sites around the state still need to be cleaned up. Government programs have led to increased recycling, but New York still produces and discards mountains of garbage each day. The state is also struggling to work with other states and with the federal government to reduce outside sources of pollution, such as acid rain caused by coal-burning power plants located hundreds of miles away in the Midwest.

It will take many years and millions of dollars to clean up all the past pollution and find the best ways to prevent future contamination. But New York is meeting the challenge with a serious commitment to protecting its rich natural resources and creating a cleaner, safer environment for everyone.

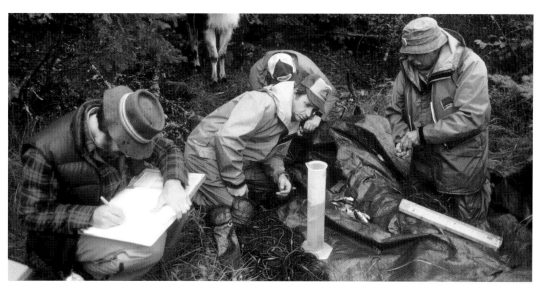

Scientists work deep in the Adirondack wilderness, gathering information on acid rain. Pollutants that fall to Earth as acid rain can be harmful to plants, wildlife, and people.

Chapter Two

The Path to Empire

Twelve thousand years ago, much of North America was covered by glaciers. During this Ice Age, ancient peoples known as Paleo-Indians traveled across a land bridge connecting Asia and North America. The Paleo-Indians were hunters, pursuing herds of woolly mammoths, mastodons, and other large game. They became the first of many settlers in the land that would one day be known as New York.

NATIVE PEOPLES

Around 8000 B.C.E. the earth's climate began to warm. The glaciers melted, covering the land bridge with ocean waters. Many of the large land animals became extinct. North America's prehistoric settlers turned to hunting smaller animals and to gathering roots, nuts, berries, and other food from wild plants.

Around 500 B.C.E. New York's native peoples learned to produce a more steady food supply through farming. Groups of hunters and farmers began to settle in permanent villages. Their population grew,

This nineteenth-century painting depicts Indians transporting furs through the North American wilderness.

developing into many separate tribes, which often battled over land and resources.

By the 1300s New York was home to two large groups of peoples descended from the ancient Paleo-Indians. The Algonquians lived mainly in the southeast, in what is now Long Island and the Hudson River valley. Algonquian tribes included the Mahican, Montauk, Wappinger, Delaware, and Lenape. The Iroquois lived farther north and west. The five Iroquois nations were the Mohawk, Oneida, Onondaga, Cayuga, and Seneca.

When the Algonquians and Iroquois battled, the Iroquois usually won. That was partly because they were such fierce warriors. The main source of the Iroquois' overwhelming power, however, was unity. According to tradition, around 1570 a warrior named Hiawatha grew sick of the constant fighting and bloodshed among the Iroquois peoples. He called a meeting of the warring chiefs. The five nations agreed to unite under a Great Tree of Peace. Their union became known as the Iroquois League, the most powerful force in North America.

Each Iroquois nation elected leaders called sachems to attend a governing council. At council

This portrait of the Oneida chief Daniel Bread was painted by the famous American artist George Catlin.

How Bear Lost His Tail: An Iroquois Story

In the old days, Bear had a long black tail. He liked to wave it about for everyone to admire. When that old trickster Fox saw this, he laughed. He decided to play a trick on Bear.

It was wintertime, when Hatho, the Spirit of Frost, covers the lakes with ice. Fox made a hole in the ice. He surrounded the hole with fish. Just as Bear walked by, Fox dipped his tail in the water and pulled out a juicy trout.

"Would you like to try?" Fox asked.

"Oh yes," said Bear.

"Then come, Brother, we will find you a good spot."

Fox knew that fish stay in deep waters when Hatho covers their lakes. He made a hole in the ice where the water was shallow. He told Bear to place his tail in the water. He said, "Do not look and do not move. When a fish grabs your tail, I will shout."

Fox sneaked home and went to bed. In the morning he returned. He laughed when he saw a small black hill, covered with snow, snoring. Quietly, he crept near. "Bear! Now!" he shouted.

Bear woke up with a start. He pulled his tail with all his strength. But the lake had frozen over, and his tail broke off—snap! Bear turned to see the beautiful fish he had caught. Instead, he saw his long black tail, caught in the ice.

So it is that today Bear has a short tail and no love for Fox. Sometimes you may even hear a bear moaning in the forests, when he thinks of his beautiful lost tail.

meetings the sachems talked over problems and disagreements. Their decisions helped keep their confederacy united and strong.

Only men could be sachems. Iroquois men were also warriors and hunters. Armed with stone clubs and bows and arrows, they searched the forests for deer, moose, bear, and other meat. The women planted and harvested corn, beans, and squash, and they gathered wild nuts and berries from the forests. In some ways Iroquois women held more power than the men. They owned all the land and property. They also decided which sachems could speak in council.

Council meetings took place around the fire in an Iroquois longhouse. Each of these large barn-shaped buildings of log and bark was home to twenty or more families. One or two families occupied a small compartment, with bark-lined beds and storage shelves. On winter days parents and children liked to gather around the fire in the long center aisle to hear an elder tell the ancient stories of their people.

THE EUROPEAN INVASION

"We found a very pleasant place, situated amongst certain little steep hills, and there ran down into the sea a great river." That is how Italian explorer Giovanni da Verrazano, the first white person ever to see New York, described his 1524 "discovery" of its sparkling harbor. After a quick look, Verrazano headed back to sea. Later visitors from Europe would stay longer, changing life in the region forever.

French explorer Samuel de Champlain hiked south from Canada in 1609. Beside the large lake later named Lake Champlain, he claimed the northern region's woods and waters for France. That same year Henry Hudson, an Englishman working for the Dutch, sailed his ship, the *Half Moon*, through New York's harbor and up a majestic river. Hudson was searching

Henry Hudson trades with native peoples in New York. The English explorer was seeking the Northwest Passage, a waterway from Europe to Asia, when he sailed up what is now called the Hudson River.

for a shortcut through North America to Asia. He was disappointed when he came to the river's end. Still, he brought back news of friendly native peoples who were willing to trade furs for guns and whiskey.

By the mid-1600s Dutch trading posts lined "Hudson's river." The most important were Fort Orange and New Amsterdam. Fort Orange was a small, rough village 150 miles upriver. Muddy New Amsterdam sat at the mouth of the Hudson, on the island Native Americans called Man-a-hat-ta, or "island of hills." Most Native Americans (the Europeans called them Indians) welcomed the Dutch. The Algonquians of Manhattan Island and the

Iroquois near Fort Orange were glad to trade their furs for the settlers' guns, blankets, liquor, and other goods.

In 1664 four British warships sailed into New Amsterdam harbor. Dutch governor Peter Stuyvesant—known as Peg Leg Pete for his wooden leg—protested the intrusion but surrendered the valuable seaport without a shot. Fort Orange was renamed Albany, in honor of the Duke of York and Albany, later King James II of England. The village of New Amsterdam and the new British colony itself were called New York.

Dutch governor Peter Stuyvesant, wearing his wooden leg and a defiant scowl, surrenders New Amsterdam to the British.

The British were bitter rivals of not only the Dutch but also the French. In 1754 Britain and France went to war over control of North America. Many of the battles of the French and Indian War were fought in New York. The Iroquois supported their trading partners, the British. The Algonquians, whose numbers had been greatly reduced by disease and warfare, sided with the French. The hard-fought war ended with the defeat of France in 1763.

DIVIDED AND UNITED

Who were the New Yorkers who witnessed Britain's victory over France in 1763? Like New Yorkers today, they were an astonishing mix of different ethnic groups.

New York colony had always attracted settlers from many lands. There were the French, Dutch, and English. There were also people from Sweden, Germany, Ireland, Scotland, Finland, Spain, and Denmark. New Englanders, known as Yankees, moved down from Connecticut and Massachusetts.

Many of these people came to New York for its religious tolerance. In their homelands they could not practice their faiths freely. New York, on the other hand, followed the traditions of the Dutch government that had founded it, welcoming Protestants, Quakers, Catholics, and Jews.

Tolerance did not mean that people always got along. Many business and religious groups battled over differing interests. Small farmers quarreled with the rich landowners who controlled all the best farmland. By the 1700s three-quarters of all New Yorkers were farmers, working plots of land rented from the colony's thirty or so wealthiest families. Other New Yorkers made their living through a trade or handicraft. There were bakers, barbers, and blacksmiths. Cobblers made shoes, coopers made barrels, and merchants bought and sold goods.

Despite their differences, these early settlers had many things in common. Nearly everyone lived in a small slice of eastern New York, within a few miles of the Hudson River or New York Harbor. Most people depended on the waterways for transporting goods. All of the settlers feared the Iroquois who controlled the western wilderness. And in the years following the French and Indian War, a new concern united New Yorkers: a growing dissatisfaction with British rule.

Wounded scouts rest in camp during the French and Indian War. The war, which lasted from 1754 to 1763, gave the British control of most of North America, including New York.

REVOLUTION'S BATTLEGROUND

The long wars with France had been costly for the British. To help pay the bill, they came up with new taxes for their American colonies. In protest, angry New Yorkers led the other colonists in a boycott, in which people refused to buy British goods. Their efforts were successful. Some of the taxes were canceled. But it was too late for compromise. Colonists who had grown tired of British control were ready to fight for independence.

One-third of the battles of the American Revolution were fought in New York. Britain's war strategy depended on separating the northern and southern colonies. New York, located in the middle of the two regions, was the key to that plan. In 1776, soon after Americans drafted their Declaration of Independence, British troops captured New York City. They would hold that prize until the end of the war.

Meanwhile, important battles raged in northern New York, including the Battle of Saratoga in 1777. This conflict in the tiny town of Saratoga ended in the colonists' first major victory. It also marked a turning point in the Revolution. The victory convinced the French that the colonists

British general John Burgoyne surrenders to American general Horatio Gates at the Battle of Saratoga in 1777.

had a good chance of winning their fight. France signed a treaty recognizing American independence and pledging to fight alongside the young nation "as good and faithful allies."

Not all Americans supported the fight for independence. New York had more Loyalists (British supporters) than any other colony. Most Loyalists lived in British-held New York City. Many of the Iroquois also remained loyal to their old trading partners. After Iroquois warriors under British command attacked New York settlements, General George Washington sent troops to take revenge. American soldiers burned Indian villages and fields, smashing the Iroquois so completely that their nations would never rise in power again.

In 1783 a thirteen-gun salute thundered over Manhattan. Britain had signed a peace agreement recognizing American independence. Five years later, New York approved the United States Constitution, becoming the new nation's eleventh state.

THE EMPIRE STATE

Northern farms and villages lay in ruins, and one-third of Manhattan had burned to the ground. No state suffered more from the Revolution than New York, and none bounced back so quickly.

With the defeat of the Iroquois, western New York was opened for settlement. Farmers and adventurers piled all they owned into covered wagons and headed for the wilderness. Meanwhile, the sounds of rebuilding rang out across New York City, America's temporary capital until 1790.

Growth halted during the War of 1812. This struggle between the United States and Great Britain over shipping rights lasted two years. Much of the fighting took place along the New York–Canadian border.

When the war ended, the rush for land resumed. Thousands of settlers swept west and north, carving fertile farms from forestland. Roadways were built over ancient Indian paths. Robert Fulton's new steamboat, the *Clermont,* paddled along the Hudson River. Still, a better way was needed to carry goods between New York's port and its growing frontier.

Many people laughed when Governor De Witt Clinton suggested building a waterway to connect the Great Lakes and the Atlantic Ocean. How would "Clinton's Ditch" cross more than 360 miles of forests, swamps, and mountains? In 1825 the doubters joined the cheering crowds as Clinton led a fleet of flat-bottomed barges down the Erie Canal.

The canal connected Lake Erie, on New York's western border, with Albany and the Hudson River. Now farmers could ship fruits and vegetables clear across the state and then down the Hudson to New York Harbor. Soon canal barges were carrying a variety of goods from western New York and the Midwest. In 1831 nearly one-third of all goods leaving the United States and more than half of all imports passed through New York City, the busiest port in the world.

The city's success attracted new businesses, including banks, shipbuilders, and newspapers. Towns along the Erie Canal also mushroomed into thriving centers of industry. Among the biggest and busiest cities were Buffalo, Rochester, Syracuse, and Utica, where factories processed wheat and other products.

By 1850 New York had about three million people, more than any other state. It was the nation's leader in manufacturing and trade. Many people called New York the crown of the growing American empire.

LOW BRIDGE! EVERYBODY DOWN

(Fifteen years on the Erie Canal)

Barges carrying passengers and freight along the Erie Canal were towed by mules, which strolled along at a leisurely rate.

By Thomas S. Allen

We better be on our way old pal,
Fifteen years on the Erie Canal.
'Cause you bet your life I'd never part
    from Sal,
Fifteen years on the Erie Canal.
Get up there, mule, here comes a lock,
We'll make Rome 'bout six o'clock.
One more trip and back we'll go,
Right back home to Buffalo. *Chorus*

I don't have to call when I want my Sal,
Fifteen years on the Erie Canal;
She trots from her stall like a good old gal.
Fifteen years on the Erie Canal,
I eat my meals with Sal each day,
I eat beef and she eats hay,
She ain't so slow if you want to know,
She put the "Buff" in Buffalo. *Chorus*

In 1843 Isabelle Baumfree heard the voice of God commanding, "Go East." The freed slave from Ulster County, New York, began touring the country, speaking out for abolition (the ending of slavery) under the name Sojourner Truth.

From its earliest days, New York had been home to a large population of slaves brought from the West Indies and Africa. When the United States took its first census in 1790, there were more than 21,000 slaves in New York, more than in some southern states. Then, in 1827, the state government passed a law ending slavery. In the years that followed, New Yorkers led the nation in the fight for abolition.

Not everyone supported abolition. In 1863, during the Civil War, mobs in New York City assaulted African Americans and burned their homes and schools. The rioters were angry about a new draft law that permitted well-to-do men to buy their way out of the service. They also resented being forced to risk their lives fighting to free the slaves. Despite the conflicts between pro- and anti-abolition forces, New York sent more soldiers to the North's Union army than any other state. Its farms and factories also contributed wheat, weapons, and other war supplies.

Born into slavery in New York, Sojourner Truth became one of the most dynamic leaders of the abolition movement.

The years from the Civil War's end in 1865 to the beginning of the twentieth century were known as the Gilded Age. In this period of growth and prosperity, new industries multiplied. Factories churned out iron, steel, clothing, glassware, magazines, and electrical equipment. New York City's Isaac Singer developed the first commercially successful sewing machine. Elisha Otis of Yonkers started a company to manufacture his new electric elevator. Rochester prospered as its factories turned out George Eastman's new handheld Kodak cameras.

This outpouring of products was largely the work of newcomers from foreign shores. In the 1830s and 1840s, immigrants had poured into the United States from Ireland and Germany. After 1880 a new wave arrived, including Italians, Greeks, and Polish and Russian Jews. Attracting all these people was America's promise of religious tolerance and financial

opportunity. Millions passed through New York Harbor, the gateway to America, and many stayed on to make New York their home. By 1900 one-third of all New Yorkers had been born in another country.

Life was not easy for these newcomers. Many worked seven days a week in filthy, unsafe factories. New York City's immigrant neighborhoods were overcrowded slums, with four or five people

An Italian mother and her children join the millions of immigrants passing through New York Harbor in the 1800s.

POPULATION GROWTH: 1790–2000

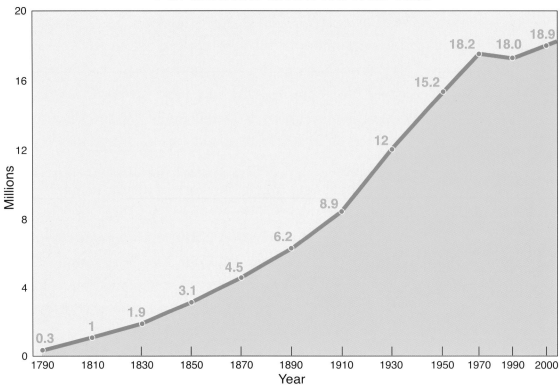

to a room. When British writer Charles Dickens visited the Irish neighborhood known as Five Points, he declared, "All that is loathsome, drooping, and decayed is here." Still, through hard work, many immigrants climbed from poverty to make good lives for themselves and their families.

Starting in 1917, more than 500,000 New Yorkers—including many immigrants and children of immigrants—fought in World War I. Wartime production kept the state's businesses booming, and many black families moved from small farms in the American South to fill factory jobs. At the war's end, soldiers were welcomed home with ticker-tape parades in New York City, the second-largest city in the world.

A street peddler sells his wares in the Lower East Side. In the late 1800s, this New York City neighborhood was home to half a million eastern European Jews.

FACING UP TO THE FUTURE

In the 1930s New York and the rest of the nation faced the period of economic hardship known as the Great Depression. The Depression began with a crisis at New York City's stock exchange, where shares in the ownership of U.S. businesses were bought and sold. In 1929 stock prices suddenly fell sharply. Stockholders lost millions of dollars, and many businesses across the country were forced to shut down. One-third of New York's male workers, along with millions of other Americans, lost their jobs. President Franklin D. Roosevelt, a native New Yorker, helped Americans through these desperate times. Roosevelt's New Deal programs created jobs and fed the needy.

Unemployed New Yorkers who have been left homeless by the Great Depression line up for food and shelter.

By the 1940s the Great Depression had ended, and America's economy revived as factories geared up for World War II. New York manufactured an incredible twenty-three billion dollars' worth of planes, ships, and other materials for U.S. troops overseas.

After the war more black southerners plus immigrants from Puerto Rico, Cuba, and the West Indies came to New York. These newcomers faced great challenges. Many businesses were moving west or south, seeking lower taxes and cheaper land and labor. Cities battled unemployment, poverty, and crime. Racial tensions sometimes led to violence. In the 1970s the state's economy hit bottom, and New York City came close to bankruptcy after banks refused to lend it any more money. In October 1975 the city asked the federal government for help. A colorful New York *Daily News* headline summed up President Gerald R. Ford's response: FORD TO CITY: DROP DEAD.

Eventually the White House came through with financial backing that helped the city survive its crisis. New York lowered taxes and started an aggressive program to bring back businesses and create jobs. In the 1980s and 1990s, the state's economy rebounded. The population grew, and tourism flourished. In 2000 more than 36 million people from all over the globe visited New York City, once again hailed as the "capital of the world."

A Daily News *headline blasts President Gerald Ford's response to New York City's request for federal assistance during the budget crisis of 1975.*

On September 11, 2001, New York City was the target of the worst terrorist attack in U.S. history. Terrorists hijacked four passenger jets and crashed two of them into the Twin Towers of Manhattan's World Trade Center. Flames fed by thousands of gallons of jet fuel turned the buildings into infernos, melting their steel structures. Within two hours both towers had collapsed. Nearly 2,800 people were killed, including the planes' passengers and crew, thousands of office workers, and hundreds of firefighters, police, and other rescue workers.

While the Twin Towers burned, terrorists crashed another hijacked plane into the Pentagon, a government building outside Washington, D.C. A fourth plane, also headed toward Washington, crashed in a field in western Pennsylvania after passengers fought back against the hijackers. Altogether the September 11 attacks left nearly three thousand dead, including people from eighty nations.

New Yorkers quickly rallied to respond to the tragedy. Volunteers rushed to the World Trade Center site to support the rescue workers clearing debris and searching for survivors. Local restaurants donated food. Thousands of people lined up to donate blood. Others gave money, clothing, and supplies. "We've seen the worst of what humanity can do, but now we're seeing the best," said Linda Blackman, a volunteer delivering supplies to rescue workers. "I'll stay here until they throw me out or I pass out."

New Yorkers also shared their sorrow, outrage, and hope through makeshift memorials that sprang up all over the city. Sites in parks, outside firehouses, and along city streets overflowed with candles, flowers, photos, flags, drawings, poems, and posters. Many of the messages expressed gratitude to the city's rescue workers. At the first of

In the aftermath of the September 11 attacks, a police officer stands guard outside the New York Stock Exchange.

many funerals for fallen fire fighters, New York mayor Rudolph Giuliani proclaimed, "They are heroes. They are like the heroes we had at Pearl Harbor. Each one of them was trying to save lives."

It took more than three months to put out the flames at the World Trade Center and nearly a year to remove all the debris. Today Americans are still struggling to heal the wounds of September 11 and to adjust to life in a world that will never be quite the same again. Many have found a new spirit and resolve. "What was really attacked on September 11th," said John P. Avlon, a former aide to Mayor Giuliani, "was the idea of New York City and America itself—a beacon of freedom, diversity, and equal opportunity. . . . Our devotion to those ideals has only been strengthened by the selfless heroism we have seen. . . . Much has been taken from us, but much remains; and even in the dark, a great deal of light still shines upon the city of New York."

Chapter Three

Living Together

This is New York: The street-smart city dweller, fast talking and always on the go; the dairy farmer tending a newborn calf; the class of sixth graders studying vocabulary words in a language once foreign to many of their parents.

No state has a greater variety of people than New York. Practically every ethnic group and nationality are part of the population mix. More than 60 percent of the state's 19.2 million people are white, with family roots reaching back mainly to European countries such as Germany, Ireland, Italy, Poland, and Greece. New York is home to 3.2 million African Americans, more than any other state. There are also 2.9 million Hispanics, who trace their roots to Spanish-speaking lands; about 1 million Asian Americans; and about 172,000 Native Americans. People of every faith live in the state, including more than one-quarter of the Jews and one-eighth of the Roman Catholics in the United States.

Because of this jumble of backgrounds, there is no such thing as a typical New Yorker. People from different cultures have held on to some of their old traditions while absorbing new customs and beliefs. At times

A New York family hikes the mountains and trails of the Adirondacks.

47

conflicts flare up between the many races, nationalities, and religions. Overall, though, New Yorkers have an unusual tolerance for different ways of life. "See these hands?" said Brooklyn barber Mehrba Kahn. "The Jews, the Christians, the Muslims here, they're like these fingers. They work together because they have to. We're all connected."

"ETHNIC SALAD"

New York has always been a melting pot. As early as the 1640s, the people of the small Dutch trading post at New Amsterdam spoke eighteen different languages. By the late 1800s, New York City had the largest immigrant workforce in the world.

A group of schoolgirls enjoys the United American Muslim Day Parade in New York City.

Immigrants often settled in separate communities because they felt more comfortable surrounded by neighbors who shared the same language and background. Visitors to nineteenth-century New York City described walking for blocks without hearing a word of English. Fifty years ago, in small towns and villages scattered throughout the state, German, Italian, Polish, Greek, and other languages were still spoken more often than English.

Even today, parts of New York can seem a world away from the rest of the country. One tourist from Denver, Colorado, summed up his visit to New York City in 2000 as "a trip around the world, without the passport and shots." The city has ethnic neighborhoods with names such as Chinatown, Little Korea, Little India, and Little Italy. El Barrio, or Spanish Harlem, is home to many of the city's Puerto Rican immigrants. In the early 1900s, more than 300,000 Jewish immigrants lived in the Lower East Side neighborhood. Today shop names and notices in Hebrew alternate with signs in Chinese and Spanish, reflecting the changing face of this community.

While New York still has many ethnic neighborhoods, today in most communities people of different backgrounds are mixed together like ingredients in a giant salad bowl. Each group is part of the whole colorful concoction while adding its own unique "flavor."

The state's richly diverse communities often celebrate their special character in festivals brought by immigrants from their homelands. The people of Germantown, North Creek, and other towns with large German-American populations enjoy annual Oktoberfests. These festivals feature folk dancing, German oompah bands, and plenty of knockwurst and sauerkraut. Italians in Brooklyn honor the Feast of Saint Paulinus of Nola in much the same way as their relatives in Nola, Italy.

Haroset Balls with Apple

Haroset is a traditional food served during the Jewish festival of Passover. Immigrants from Spain brought this recipe for haroset to New York three hundred years ago. Dates were used in the original recipe, but in New York apples make the perfect substitute.

1. Place 3 cups raisins and 1½ cups blanched almonds in a bowl. Chop them into tiny pieces.*
2. Peel ½ apple and remove the core. Slice the apple and add it to the raisins and almonds.
3. Add ½ teaspoon cinnamon.
4. Finely chop the mixture to make a lumpy paste.
5. Shape the paste into balls about the size of large marbles.
6. Press one whole blanched almond on top of each haroset ball.

Makes about 48 haroset balls.
*Be sure to ask an adult to help when you use sharp knives.

While crowds of onlookers cheer, men dance through the streets carrying the *giglio* (JEE-lee-oh), an eighteen-foot tower covered with flowers and topped with the saint's statue. The Welsh Barn Festival in Remsen features the *Gymanfa Ganu,* a Welsh hymn-sing dating back more than 150 years. New Yorkers of Scottish heritage celebrate the yearly Capital District Scottish Games in Altamont, outside Albany.

It takes one hundred people to carry the towering giglio *of Saint Paulinus through the streets of Brooklyn during the Italian-American festival honoring the saint.*

The highlight of this festival is a parade of marching bands, with hundreds of bagpipe musicians proudly wearing the kilts and colors of their ancient family clans.

CHANGING BLACK NEIGHBORHOODS

Many black New Yorkers make their homes in small towns and villages. The majority, however, live in the cities. Nearly three-quarters of New York's 3.2 million African Americans reside in New York City.

These settlement patterns can be traced back to the early 1900s. Large numbers of southern blacks came to New York in that period, finding jobs in major manufacturing centers such as Buffalo, Rochester, and, of course, New York City. Large black communities grew up in Brooklyn and in a part of northern Manhattan known as Harlem.

In the 1920s Harlem was an exciting place, a center of culture and entertainment. During what is known as the Harlem Renaissance, black writers, composers, and other artists gained an enthusiastic audience for their celebrations of African-American culture. People came from miles around to Harlem's theaters and nightclubs to enjoy performances by great black actors, singers, and jazz orchestras.

In Mount Vernon, three generations trace their family's history through the pages of an old photo album.

The Harlem Renaissance faded with the Great Depression. After World War II, blacks in Harlem and other city neighborhoods were hit hard by job and housing shortages. Many whites began moving out of the cities to the suburbs. As whites moved out, many poor blacks moved in, filling low-income public housing projects. The "projects" were often haunted by unemployment, poverty, crime, and drugs. Some of the people living in these crowded buildings felt angry and frustrated, with little hope for the future.

Racial tensions have sometimes led to violence. Between 1935 and 1977, there were five race riots in Harlem. In 1989 rioters attacked police in Brooklyn after black teenager Yusef Hawkins was killed by a gang of young white men. Brooklyn was the site of further turmoil in 1991, when a conflict between Orthodox (strictly religious) Jews and black residents touched off several days of rioting.

Today New York City's historically black neighborhoods are mixed scenes of poverty and despair, revival and hope. Some children growing up in public housing projects remain trapped in a cycle of poverty. "We have a short expectancy in life," said Elliott Wilson, who grew up in a project in Queens, "so we go for the quick buck. That's why kids sell drugs. That's why they rob. We don't feel we can be on a five-year plan to success."

At the same time, the crime rate is down significantly in New York City, and it has dropped even more sharply in housing developments than in the city as a whole. Neighborhoods such as Harlem are enjoying what some people call a "Second Renaissance," with thriving clubs, theaters, churches, and restaurants. Many middle-class African Americans who had left the city are returning to live and invest in their old neighborhoods. High-school teacher Michelle Robinson "saw so much craziness" growing

Despite occasional tensions, most New Yorkers of different nationalities, ethnic backgrounds, and faiths live side by side in peace and friendship.

up in Brooklyn's working-class Bedford-Stuyvesant section that she vowed to "go to a good college, make some money and never ever return back to the 'hood." Recently, Robinson left the suburbs and returned home. "This is where I need to be," she said. "Our neighborhoods [are] cleaner and there are more business opportunities than when I was growing up."

City neighborhoods are also becoming more racially diverse. William Etheridge grew up in a section of Queens that was once overwhelmingly black. He recently moved back to find "a rainbow of diversity—Asians, blacks, and whites." Many of the newcomers to these changing neighborhoods are well educated and middle class. Some people worry that their presence will drive up rents and prices, pushing out long-time residents and small businesses. Others applaud the changes and work to find compromises that will allow old and new to live side by side. "We need to co-exist," said Thelma Russell, director of the Harlem Business Alliance, "and I think you can have them both. Everyone has to stick together."

A young girl prepares to celebrate her heritage in Brooklyn's annual Caribbean Children's Parade.

Immigration Issues

In 2000 New York had nearly four million foreign-born residents, an increase of about one-third since 1990. During the same ten-year period, more than 30,000 native-born New Yorkers left the state. The result: nearly every county lost white residents and gained people of African, Asian, and Hispanic descent.

That booming immigrant population has brought serious challenges. Immigrants who do not speak English require special services in schools and other institutions. Foreign-born New Yorkers are more likely than native-born residents to live in poverty and to require public assistance such as food stamps and welfare. The state also pays out millions of dollars each year in emergency medical care for tens of thousands of immigrants without health insurance. New York's share of all these costs skyrocketed after federal welfare reform laws were passed in 1996, making vast numbers of immigrants ineligible for federal assistance programs.

At the same time, there are many advantages to New York's growing immigrant population. Recent studies have shown that naturalized citizens (legal immigrants who become citizens) make more money and pay more in taxes the longer they live in the state. After fifteen years New York's naturalized citizens earn slightly more than native-born residents and are less likely to receive welfare.

Immigration is also "a lifeblood of new population," said research scientist Dr. William Frey. Without it, many communities would be shrinking. Instead, new generations of New Yorkers "are revitalizing and re-energizing these neighborhoods."

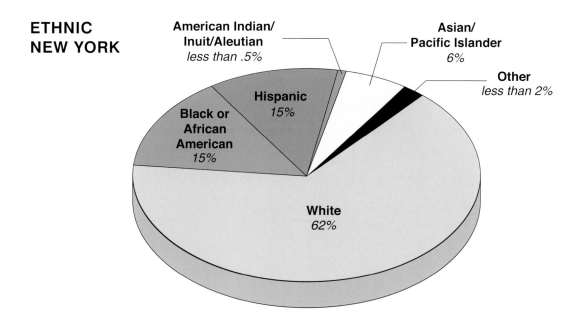

ETHNIC NEW YORK

American Indian/ Inuit/Aleutian
less than .5%

Asian/ Pacific Islander
6%

Other
less than 2%

Hispanic
15%

Black or African American
15%

White
62%

HISPANIC COMMUNITIES

Hispanic New Yorkers come from a variety of backgrounds. Their families have emigrated from Puerto Rico, the Dominican Republic, Mexico, Colombia, El Salvador, Cuba, and other Spanish-speaking countries. Like African Americans, Hispanic New Yorkers live in communities all over the state, with the majority in the larger cities. About three-quarters live in New York City.

Piri Thomas grew up among the "hustles and rackets" of the Manhattan neighborhood known as Spanish Harlem. He wrote about the neighborhood's dirt and noise, the "crying kids, hustlers, dogs yapping, and cats making holes in mountains of garbage." Poverty, unemployment, crime, and drug abuse have long been serious problems in Spanish Harlem and many other Hispanic communities. Parents who came to the United States hoping to make a better life for their families often could not find good jobs or housing. They worry when their children witness

A city sidewalk becomes an obstacle course for this daring young skateboarder.

gang violence and drug dealing on the streets.

Today as many as half of New York City's Hispanics live in poverty. They are more likely than black or white New Yorkers to receive welfare, live in substandard housing, and attend low-quality schools. Some of their difficulties stem from language. Schools, government offices, and other institutions have had to scramble to provide services to the rapidly growing population of Spanish-speaking New Yorkers. Meanwhile, community leaders work hard to bring new hope and opportunities to Hispanic neighborhoods.

David Cutié and his wife, Betty, left Spanish Harlem fifteen years ago to raise their daughter in the suburbs. They returned in 2003 to find a changed community. "The streets are safer," said Cutié. "The streets are cleaner." New and renovated buildings offer cultural attractions unheard-of just a few years ago, including museums, youth centers, concerts, art exhibits, and poetry readings.

Dominican immigrant Astin Jacobo has also seen his neighborhood in the Bronx rise from the ashes. Ten years ago, fires raced through crumbling slum tenements. The streets were like a war zone, filled with rubble, broken glass, and the crack of gunshots from gangs and drug dealers. Jacobo and a handful of other community activists organized their neighbors. They pressed city officials to convert crumbling apartment buildings into low-rent housing and to build modest two- and three-family brick row houses on vacant lots. They planted a community garden and put in baseball and soccer fields. Now new homes, businesses, and families are bringing the neighborhood back to life. "There is a return to green," said Jacobo. "We're emerging. We're seeing things return to the way it should be."

Hispanic New Yorkers know that there is still a long way to go before they achieve their goal of ensuring a good future for their children. Population experts predict that continuing immigration from Spanish-speaking lands will soon make Hispanics the country's "majority minority." "We have to be careful because we are the majority in people but not in

A three-year-old clutches a Mexican flag at the annual Mexican Day Parade in the Manhattan borough of Queens.

power," said Jacobo. "We have to be the majority . . . not just in quantity but in quality. In education, business, politics, well-being. We have to open up to other communities."

ASIAN NEW YORKERS

Like other immigrant groups, most Asian Americans came to the United States in search of a better life. In recent years people from China, Korea, Japan, the Philippines, Bangladesh, India, Pakistan, and other Asian countries have been New York's fastest-growing immigrant group. Three-quarters of Asian New Yorkers live in New York City, mostly in the borough of Queens and in Manhattan's Chinatown.

Chinatown is home to nearly five thousand Chinese Americans. Colorful banners stretch across this lively neighborhood's narrow, winding streets. Tourists flock to the shops for bargains on everything from teapots to chopsticks to kung fu swords. On Chinese New Year, Chinatown's main street overflows with Chinese New Yorkers in colorful costumes, celebrating in a shower of fireworks.

In Chinatown the biggest holiday of the year is Chinese New Year. This man is dressed as the "monkey king" to welcome the Year of the Monkey, 2004 (or 4702, according to the Chinese calendar).

Asian New Yorkers often have more education and higher incomes than other immigrant groups. Their success has sometimes led to friction. For example, Korean Americans living in New York City have opened thousands of busy groceries and other small businesses, often in black and Hispanic neighborhoods. Some Korean storekeepers do not trust their black customers, while some African Americans refuse to shop in Korean stores. In 1990 African-American Brooklynites staged a nine-month boycott of a Korean-owned grocery store after the owner accused a black customer of shoplifting. More recently grocers in Manhattan have been boycotted and picketed by Hispanic protestors who accused the Koreans of forcing Mexican employees to work in poor conditions for low pay. Some storeowners have responded by raising wages and shortening workdays. Others are leaving the business. "There's too much damage in my community," said merchant Jae Il Kim. "Everybody's scared."

Another reality confronting Asian Americans in New York City is gang violence. Street gangs of young Asian immigrants rob homes and businesses or make storeowners pay "lucky" money to avoid being robbed. These gangs generally target fellow Asians. "Recent Asian immigrants are more likely to keep their valuables . . . in their house or business," explained Vietnamese-American social scientist C. N. Le. Also, because they often do not trust the police, "Asian Americans are the least likely to report violent crimes."

The key to many of the challenges facing immigrants is language. More than one-quarter of Asian New Yorkers speak little or no English. In many homes families speak two languages. Daniel Kim emigrated from Korea in 1987 and had his first English lesson in seventh grade. At home, he said, "even if the sentence starts out in English, it'll end

A young boy from Thailand dresses in traditional clothing from his native land during a festival celebrating New York City's rich ethnic diversity.

in Korean." While first-generation immigrants struggle, their children usually learn English quickly and become a "bridge" between the older generation and life in their new homelands.

NEW YORK'S NATIVE HERITAGE

Most of New York's 172,000 Native Americans live on Indian reservations and in large cities, especially New York City. Reservations are lands that were set apart by the U.S. government, starting in the late 1700s, as treaties forced Native Americans off their ancient lands. The Iroquois have nine reservations in New York, belonging to tribes from nations including the Seneca, Cayuga, Onondaga, Oneida, Tuscarora, and St. Regis Mohawks. Two Algonquian tribes also have their own reservations.

Today many reservations struggle with poverty, unemployment, and overcrowding. In recent years some have raised money by building casinos on reservation lands, where state gambling laws do not apply. Some Indians have welcomed the casinos and the strength that comes with prosperity. "We had tried poverty for two hundred years," said Ray Halbritter, an Oneida leader who helped establish the first Iroquois casino in New York. "We decided to try something else. . . . He who has the gold makes the rules." Others are concerned that embracing the materialism and greed of white society will destroy their traditional culture and values.

A Seneca Indian boy wears a traditional ceremonial costume. Nearly ten thousand members of the Seneca Nation of Indians live on three reservations in western New York.

To preserve their ancient heritage, the people of New York's Indian reservations have set up educational programs, libraries, and museums. Schoolchildren learn the languages and customs of their ancestors. Annual festivals also help preserve the past. The Seneca Indian Fall Festival, held each September at the Cattaraugus Indian Reservation in western New York, is a lively event featuring traditional music, dance, arts, crafts, foods, and games.

It is more difficult for Native Americans who live in the cities to remain connected with their heritage. Rosemary Richmond, a Mohawk who grew up in Westchester County, just north of New York City, is the director of the American Indian Community House in Manhattan. Her organization provides health, housing, and job assistance to the needy and operates a cultural center, bookstore, and art gallery. "A lot of people think Indians are only historical figures in movies and books," said Richmond. "The concept of Indian people as feathers and beads and wars, that's not all there is."

UPSTATE VERSUS DOWNSTATE

Along with the differences among New York's ethnic groups, another wide gap divides New Yorkers. That is the gulf between people living in the regions known as upstate and downstate. No set line on a map defines these regions. To most people, "upstate" means any area north of New York City and its suburbs, while the city and its nearby communities, including Long Island and the lower Hudson Valley, are "downstate."

The downstate region has a larger and more diverse population. It includes more low-income people who depend on social services. It is also home to the majority of New York's African Americans, Hispanics, Asians, Democrats, and Jews. The majority of upstaters are white, Republican, and Protestant. They often think of downstaters as having different

POPULATION DISTRIBUTION

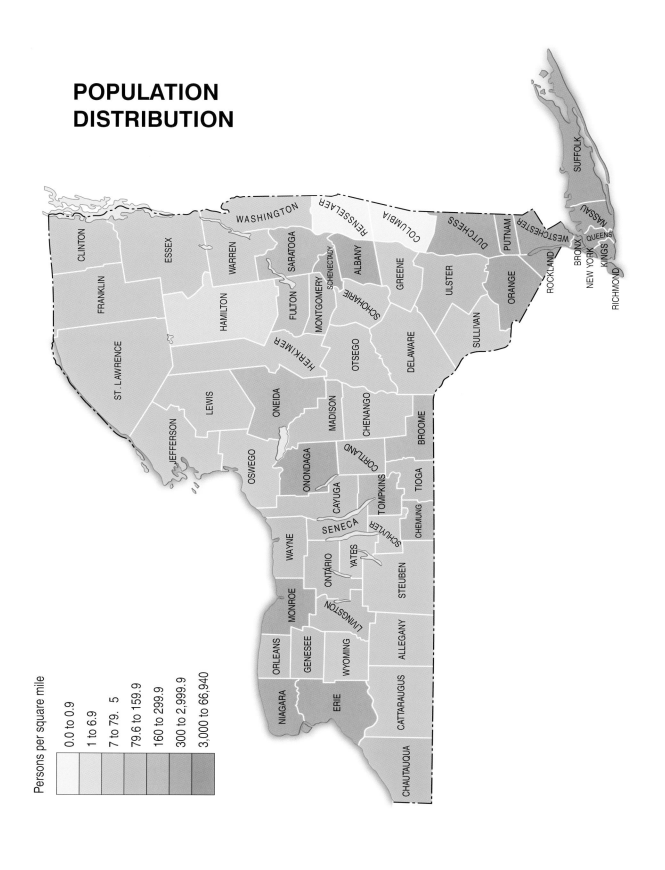

Persons per square mile

0.0 to 0.9
1 to 6.9
7 to 79. 5
79.6 to 159.9
160 to 299.9
300 to 2,999.9
3,000 to 66,940

CLINTON
ESSEX
WASHINGTON
RENSSELAER
COLUMBIA
DUTCHESS
PUTNAM
WESTCHESTER
SUFFOLK
NASSAU
QUEENS
BRONX
NEW YORK
KINGS
RICHMOND
ROCKLAND
ORANGE
ULSTER
GREENE
ALBANY
SCHENECTADY
SARATOGA
WARREN
FRANKLIN
HAMILTON
FULTON
MONTGOMERY
SCHOHARIE
SULLIVAN
DELAWARE
OTSEGO
HERKIMER
ST. LAWRENCE
LEWIS
ONEIDA
MADISON
CHENANGO
BROOME
JEFFERSON
OSWEGO
ONONDAGA
CORTLAND
TIOGA
CAYUGA
TOMPKINS
CHEMUNG
SCHUYLER
SENECA
WAYNE
ONTARIO
YATES
STEUBEN
MONROE
LIVINGSTON
ORLEANS
GENESEE
WYOMING
ALLEGANY
NIAGARA
ERIE
CATTARAUGUS
CHAUTAUQUA

concerns from their own, and they may suspect that downstate gets more than its fair share of federal and state dollars.

From time to time, disputes between the two regions have even led to proposals to divide New York into two states. "Every so often," said northern New Yorker John Rathbone, "there is a hue and cry to create a new 51st state. Sometimes it is Upstaters who call for this, sometimes it is Downstaters. In almost three quarters of a century, I've seen it both ways!"

Recent years have brought some changes to this age-old rivalry. Many black, Hispanic, and Asian New Yorkers have moved north, bringing greater ethnic variety to upstate towns and cities. Between 1990 and 2000, for example, the African-American population of the upstate city of Rochester increased by 15 percent, while the Hispanic population grew by 44 percent. At the same time, thousands of New Yorkers, both upstate and downstate, have moved from cities and farm towns to the growing suburbs. As people from different backgrounds and ethnic groups come together, the sharp line dividing upstate and downstate has begun to blur.

"New York is not a finished culture," wrote historian David Ellis. "It is one

A fisherman patiently waits for a bite on a frozen lake in upstate New York.

continually coming into being." Hardworking people have brought the culture and traditions of many lands to New York. The challenges of putting all their different talents to work and learning to live together make New York a strong, vibrant, and ever-changing state.

Old-Time Tales

Many of the traditional stories of New York State are tall tales, or exaggerated stories about the adventures of local heroes. In Saratoga County, north of Albany, old-timers still tell tales about a famous local lumberman named Bill Greenfield. Bill was a real person, born in 1833, who seems to have been largely responsible for his own fame. He liked to make up adventures featuring himself as the hero. Many of his tales were borrowed from old stories told by his Scottish grandfather.

According to the stories, Bill was a big man with a giant appetite. When the lumber camp's cook couldn't make enough pancakes to satisfy him, Bill built a new griddle that was 235 feet wide. To grease the giant pan, men strapped slabs of bacon on their feet and skated across its surface.

Around Bill even the weather could be remarkable. One winter it got so cold that he had to pound the frozen air into pieces just to breathe it. When he built a fire, the flames froze in a column forty feet high. Bill and his father took shelter in a cave, but when they tried to talk, their words froze solid. The next Fourth of July, Bill returned to the same cave alone and was surprised to hear his dad's voice, just thawing out, saying, "Here, Bill, have a drink."

Chapter Four

Head and Heart

New York's budget, or spending plan, in 2005 was $105 billion. That's greater than the budget of many foreign nations. More than 19 million New Yorkers from different regions, ethnic groups, and economic classes have an interest in how that money is spent. Many of them produce the goods and services that help keep the state financially strong. One of government's jobs is to build the state's economy so that New York will continue to grow and attract new businesses. Government also has the responsibility to make sure that New Yorkers with differing interests have a fair say in how their state is run.

INSIDE GOVERNMENT

The government of New York, like that of the nation, is divided into three independent branches: executive, legislative, and judicial.

Executive Branch

The head of the executive branch is the governor, who is elected to a four-year term, after which he or she can be re-elected. New York's governor appoints judges and department heads, prepares the state budget, proposes

The New York State legislature meets in the Capitol building in Albany. When this $25 million structure was completed in 1899, it was the most expensive government building of its time.

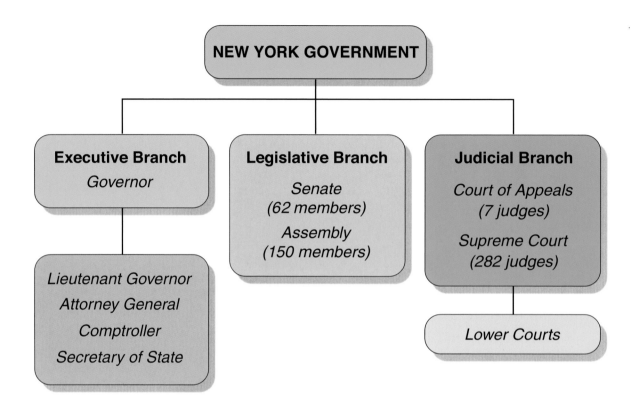

New York Government

Executive Branch
Governor

Lieutenant Governor
Attorney General
Comptroller
Secretary of State

Legislative Branch
Senate
(62 members)
Assembly
(150 members)

Judicial Branch
Court of Appeals
(7 judges)
Supreme Court
(282 judges)

Lower Courts

legislation, and can veto or reject proposed laws. It is a powerful position, and over the years New Yorkers have chosen high-powered leaders to fill it.

Four New York governors have become U.S. presidents: Martin Van Buren, Grover Cleveland, Theodore Roosevelt, and Franklin D. Roosevelt. Van Buren started studying law at age fourteen and won his first case two years later. Cleveland was a hardworking president who often stayed at his desk until two or three in the morning. Theodore Roosevelt became famous during the Spanish-American War when he led his Rough Riders—a gang of cowboys and football players—in a charge up San Juan Hill in Cuba. Franklin Roosevelt was thirty-nine when he contracted the disease polio, which left his legs permanently paralyzed. Seven years later, he ran for

Martin Van Buren was New York's ninth governor and the eighth president of the United States.

governor and won. As president, Roosevelt led Americans through the Great Depression and World War II, assuring them, "The only thing we have to fear is fear itself."

Mario Cuomo served as governor from 1983 to 1995. The son of Italian immigrants, this Democrat led the state through two periods of economic crisis. Cuomo started progressive social service programs including the nation's most extensive drug treatment network, largest program for the mentally ill, and largest housing assistance program for the homeless.

Conservative Republican George Pataki was elected as governor in 1994, pledging to "reduce the costs, the burdens and the intrusions of government." Pataki has worked to spur economic growth, protect the environment, and improve health care for children. His popularity soared as a result of his leadership following the World Trade Center attacks in 2001, and he was re-elected for a third term in 2002.

New York's governors are assisted in their duties by several top officials. The lieutenant governor, attorney general, and comptroller are just a few of the executive branch leaders who help run the state. The lieutenant governor stands ready to serve when the governor cannot. The attorney general is the state's top lawyer. The comptroller manages New York's financial records.

New York's legislature is divided into two houses: a senate with 62 members and an assembly with 150 members. Each legislator is elected for a two-year term to speak for and serve the people of a particular district, or section of the state.

The legislature's most important job is to create laws. Bills, or proposed laws, can originate in either house. They must be passed by a majority of the members of both houses. After the senate and assembly agree on a bill, it goes to the governor. If the governor signs the bill, it becomes a law. If the

The Budget Blues

One of the most important jobs of New York's governor is putting together and proposing a state budget. This plan shows what programs, groups, and agencies will receive what portion of government spending in the coming year.

The governor must submit a budget proposal to the legislature in January. Lawmakers then have until April 1 to debate, argue, negotiate, and ultimately pass an approved budget. Beginning in 1985, they missed that deadline for a record twenty years in a row. Late budgets meant major headaches for nonprofit agencies and school districts, which had to wait weeks or months to find out how much state aid would be available for their programs.

Finally, in 2005, state lawmakers worked overtime to pass the budget by the April 1 deadline. One assemblyman celebrated the event by passing out chocolate cigars with wrapping that read, "It's a Budget!"

Rallies like this demonstration outside the Capitol in Albany are one of the many ways New Yorkers make their voices heard and help shape government policies.

governor vetoes the bill, it still can become a law, but only if a two-thirds majority in both houses vote to overturn the veto.

New York's legislators represent districts with very different needs. It takes strong leadership to get them to support new legislation. The members of the two houses have traditionally granted tremendous power to their elected leaders, the senate majority leader and the speaker of the assembly. These two leaders decide on the staff and budgets of individual legislators, and they make appointments to the committees that consider bills. Some members who have refused to go along with their leadership on important issues have even found themselves locked out of their offices!

Since 1974 the Democrats have been the majority power in the assembly, and the Republicans have held the majority in the senate. To get anything accomplished, the two houses must compromise. When one house needs the other's support on a bill, the speaker of the assembly and the senate majority leader often "horse-trade." For example, in 1994 the Democratic assembly opposed the Republican senate's proposals to cut business taxes. To persuade the assembly to go along with the measure, the senate agreed to support a program favored by the Democrats, which gave New York City millions of dollars to repair public schools.

Sometimes the governor and the house leaders meet to work out compromises that will ensure passage of a bill. That has led critics to claim that "three men in a room" make all the major decisions in New York's government.

Judicial Branch

New York has one of the busiest and most complicated court systems in the nation. The highest court is the court of appeals, with a chief judge and six associate judges, all appointed by the governor. Next come the supreme court, then the appellate courts, then thousands of lower courts, which handle cases in special areas of responsibility or in specific counties, cities, towns, or villages. All these courts make decisions on matters ranging from crimes to divorces to complaints against the state.

Some New Yorkers believe that their court system is too complicated. They say that confusion over which courts should handle which cases leads to courtroom delays and crowds the jails with people awaiting trial. Overlapping court responsibilities also cause errors and unnecessary expense. "This confusing system wastes time and money," said Chief Administrative Judge E. Leo Milonas. Milonas and other judges have proposed combining some of New York's courts to make "a single, unified court" that could deliver "fair and reasonably swift justice."

NEW YORK
BY
COUNTY

CLINTON

ESSEX

FRANKLIN

WASHINGTON

RENSSELAER

COLUMBIA

WARREN

SARATOGA

DUTCHESS

PUTNAM

ST. LAWRENCE

HAMILTON

FULTON

SCHENECTADY

ALBANY

GREENE

ULSTER

ORANGE

WESTCHESTER

ROCKLAND

BRONX

SUFFOLK

NASSAU

QUEENS

NEW YORK

KINGS

RICHMOND

MONTGOMERY

SCHOHARIE

HERKIMER

OTSEGO

DELAWARE

SULLIVAN

JEFFERSON

LEWIS

ONEIDA

MADISON

CHENANGO

BROOME

OSWEGO

ONONDAGA

CORTLAND

TIOGA

CAYUGA

TOMPKINS

CHEMUNG

SENECA

SCHUYLER

WAYNE

ONTARIO

YATES

STEUBEN

MONROE

LIVINGSTON

ORLEANS

GENESEE

WYOMING

ALLEGANY

NIAGARA

ERIE

CATTARAUGUS

CHAUTAUQUA

In 1993 Chief Judge Judith Kaye of the Court of Appeals began a program to simplify New York's court system. While some of her reform proposals stalled in the legislature, the judge was able to push through many improvements. One of her innovations was a system of "specialist" courts devoted to specific types of crime. For example, many New Yorkers accused of drug-related crimes now appear before special drug courts. Instead of being sent to prison, they may be entered in drug treatment programs to fight their addictions. Social workers and court officers keep an eye on their progress, and the same judge follows their case all the way through to the completion of treatment.

GOVERNMENT'S HEART

"It is our solemn duty," said former New York governor Thomas E. Dewey, "to show that government can have both a head and a heart." New York shows its heart with generous programs that serve its citizens in need. In fact, no state spends more on public assistance programs, including education and services for the poor.

Education

Education is the state's most costly public service. In the years 2001–2002, more than 2.8 million boys and girls attended New York State's public schools. An average of nearly $11,000 a year went to educating each student. That was more than was spent by any other state.

A small portion of the money for education comes from the federal government. The rest is paid by the state and by hundreds of local school districts. School districts are like mini-governments running the schools in their area. The New York State Education Department oversees them all.

New York's school system has been called one of the best and worst in the nation. A high proportion of graduates have won academic awards and

Seventh graders at the Young Women's School of East Harlem gather round for science class. The experimental new school was called "one of the great success stories in single-sex public schools" after every member of its first graduating class was accepted into college.

scholarships and gone on to college. At the same time, the state has a high dropout rate, and its high-school students rank near the bottom of the nation in scores on Scholastic Assessment Tests (SATs).

One of the main reasons behind these contradictions is the vast difference in quality among the state's public schools. Most schools in wealthy districts have small classes, well-stocked libraries, and plenty of computers and other up-to-date technology. Schools in poorer districts are often overcrowded, rundown, and underequipped.

Conditions are especially bad in New York City's poorer neighborhoods. A survey in 1999 found that 40 percent of the city's schools were overcrowded. Some schools were even forced to hold some of their classes in hallways and auditoriums. Classrooms have crumbling walls and broken windows. "You have roofs that leak," said teachers' representative Randi Weingarten. "You have structural damage where bricks could possibly fall off or tumble off the exteriors of buildings." One student reported, "I was at the auditorium sitting watching a performance and I felt something run over my feet. I look down and saw a mouse; in class I saw one too."

New York's complicated system of school funding was designed to fix problems like these. Wealthy districts, which are able to raise more money from local property taxes, are supposed to receive less state aid.

2002 a state appellate court agreed. This court concluded that the state was living up to its obligations as long as every student received the equivalent of an eighth- or ninth-grade education.

That set the stage for an appeal by the Campaign for Fiscal Equity. This time the results were far different. In a landmark ruling in June 2003, the Court of Appeals reinstated Judge DeGrasse's ruling. "Students require more than an eighth-grade education to function properly as citizens," wrote Chief Judge Judith Kaye. The court gave the governor and legislature one year to make reforms providing a solid education for every school-aged child in New York City.

The decision in the Campaign for Fiscal Equity lawsuit applied only to New York City schools. Education reformers pledged to continue the fight statewide. "The time for tinkering with the school aid formula in New York State is over," said CFE director Michael Rebell. "Reform of the entire statewide education finance system is imperative."

Poorer districts should receive more. The idea is to give all children an equal chance at a good education. But it does not always work out that way. The system has not been able to keep up with the state's rapid rise in population, especially in poorer school districts. Politics has also played a major role in New York's public school problems.

Every year there is a huge battle as the governor, legislature, and school districts argue over how much of the state budget should go to education and how much of that lump sum should go to each district. When governors present their annual budgets, they almost always try to save money by proposing cuts in education spending. The budget then goes to the legislature. During the wheeling and dealing that follows, representatives from wealthier districts usually succeed in restoring the cuts to their schools. That leaves less money for upgrading the schools in poorer districts.

In recent years groups of educators and parents have called for a complete overhaul of the state's school funding system. In 2003 their efforts paid off in an historic court decision that is expected to have a major impact on New York City schools.

IT'S THE LAW

New York's government tries to balance a generous heart with a strong arm. A powerful police force—one of the largest in the nation—protects people and fights crime.

The state's crime rate has dropped steadily every year since 1990. By 2000 New York had the fortieth-highest crime rate of all the states. Over the same ten-year period, the overall crime rate in New York City fell more than 25 percent, and violent crime fell more than half.

Many people credit the city's dramatic drop in crime to "get-tough" policies begun during Mayor Rudolph Giuliani's time in office from 1994 to 2001. One of the key features of those policies was a crackdown on lower-level crimes such as breaking windows and drinking in public. "Obviously murder and graffiti are two vastly different crimes," said the mayor. "But they are part of the same continuum, and a climate that tolerates one is more likely to tolerate the other."

Another reason for the dropping crime rate, both in the city and statewide, is tough gun controls. In 2000 Governor Pataki signed into law the nation's strictest gun controls. The new program included background checks on buyers at gun shows and banned the sale or possession

A police officer takes the time to talk with a teenager in New York City. Aggressive crime prevention and crime-fighting measures have made New York one of the safest large cities in the nation.

of assault weapons. What about criminals who steal or borrow their guns? To catch them, New York City police have started searching suspicious-looking characters stopped for minor offenses. Arturo Garcia, who worked in a high-crime neighborhood, explained, "With all the police vigilance [watchfulness], nobody dares carry their guns."

New York is tough on crime in other ways, too. An act known as "Jenna's Law," passed in 1998, requires longer prison terms for persons convicted of violent crimes. In 2000 the legislature passed the Hate Crimes Act, which increases penalties for criminals who target victims because of characteristics such as race or religion. "Assaulting a man or a woman because they are a member of a particular ethnic group or religious minority or because of their sexual orientation is an attack on all New Yorkers," Governor Pataki said as he signed the legislation into law. "People who act on hate need to know their punishment will be swift, severe and just."

The state has also invested in technology that lets police investigating a crime search for clues in a statewide DNA database. DNA is a chemical structure found in the blood or other biological samples taken from convicted criminals. Because every person's DNA is different, these twenty-first century "fingerprints" can be used to link suspects to evidence found at crime scenes.

Chapter Five

An Economic Powerhouse

New York was once the largest manufacturing center in the world. In the late 1940s, more than one-third of the state's workers were employed in factories. New York City alone had some 40,000 factories, employing more than a million people.

Today manufacturing is still important, providing jobs to countless New Yorkers. The majority of the state's workers, however, are employed in industries that provide services rather than products. Service-sector businesses include banks, insurance companies, advertising agencies, real estate offices, restaurants, hotels, stores, airports, railways, and hospitals.

New York has struggled through periods of economic downturn, most notably in the 1970s and following the World Trade Center attacks on September 11, 2001. Despite the tough times, it has always survived and grown stronger. Today the state's vibrant businesses make it an economic giant, with the tenth-largest economy in the world.

An apple grower picks Macintosh apples on his farm in the Mohawk River valley of central New York. More than one-quarter of the land in New York is used for agriculture.

The heart of the state's economy beats in New York City. The city is the nation's business leader in areas that include finance, insurance, international trade, advertising, printing, and publishing.

Most businesses housed among the city skyscrapers and crowded streets are part of the service industry, especially finance and banking. Nearly every major investment bank and brokerage firm has offices on and around Wall Street in lower Manhattan. The Wall Street district is also home to the New York Stock Exchange. Millions of dollars' worth of shares in some three thousand companies are bought and sold on the exchange each day. New York's central role in the economic health of the world is summed up in an old saying: "When Wall Street sneezes, the world catches a cold."

The trading floor of the New York State Exchange is a busy, noisy, exciting place where fortunes change hands every day.

New York City is also a center of manufacturing, with some 11,000 companies employing more than 200,000 people. The city's workers lead the nation in the production of clothing as well as printed materials such as books and magazines. However, many of the city's small, old-style manufacturing jobs are dying out. "Everything is going . . . all the small industries," said Saul Gever, one of the city's few remaining shoemakers. "Handbags, shoes. . . . I feel like the last of a kind."

Service jobs dominate to the east of the city, on Long Island. Many people there work in stores, schools, hospitals, and doctors' offices. Long Island is home to a variety of companies that carry out scientific research and manufacture high-tech medical tools, electronics, and computer software.

Down the road from Long Island's modern laboratories and manufacturing facilities, neat rows of potatoes and cauliflower grow on hundreds of "truck farms." Vegetables from these small farms are trucked to New York City markets. Joining them on the highways are greenhouse flowers, farm-raised ducks, and eggs, as well as clams, oysters, and fresh fish from the salt waters of Long Island Sound.

Fishermen remove the shells from oysters gathered in the waters of Long Island Sound. The sound is an estuary—a partially enclosed body of water where freshwater from the land and rivers mixes with salty seawater.

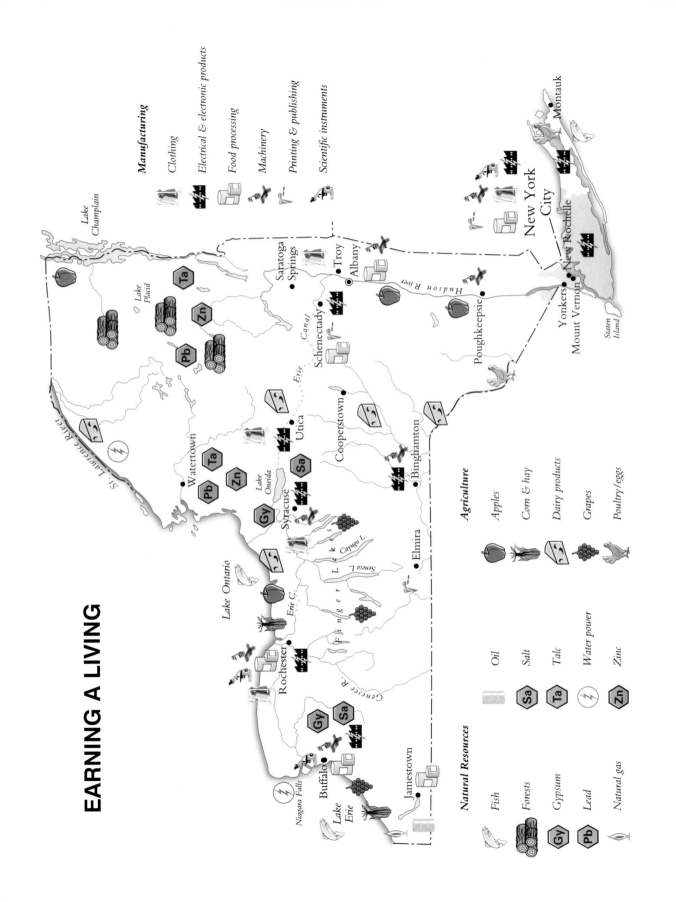

EARNING A LIVING

Manufacturing

- Clothing
- Electrical & electronic products
- Food processing
- Machinery
- Printing & publishing
- Scientific instruments

Agriculture

- Apples
- Corn & hay
- Dairy products
- Grapes
- Poultry/eggs

Natural Resources

- Fish
- Forests
- Gypsum
- Lead
- Natural gas
- Oil
- Salt
- Talc
- Water power
- Zinc

Agriculture is important along the Hudson River, too. Farmers grow vegetables and fruits, especially apples, and they raise chickens for eggs and cows for milk. Service and manufacturing industries also flourish in the Hudson Valley. Many small cities have grown up around one industry, sometimes around one company. Schenectady, birthplace of the General Electric Company, makes electrical equipment. Computer giant IBM employs thousands of people at its corporate headquarters in Armonk and at nearby research labs. In Albany government is the main employer. One out of every five workers living in the capital is employed by the state government.

BUSY CITIES, QUIET FARMS

Western New York's cities also have their specialties. Rochester manufactures photographic and optical equipment. Corning is the world leader in fiber optic wires, used in telecommunications. Buffalo, at the western end of the Erie Canal, grew to become New York's second-largest city through the milling of grain passing on its way from the Midwest to the east coast. Today this city's diverse economy includes automaking and other heavy manufacturing, dairy and agriculture, health care, and education.

A worker unloads grapes at a vineyard in western New York. Nearly 30,000 acres of the state's farmlands are used for growing grapes.

Celebrating Nature's Bounty

Sample a maple lollipop. Dig into a strawberry pizza. Join a grape-stomping contest or try to top the record for raw-oyster eating—two hundred in two minutes forty seconds—at Long Island's annual Oyster Festival. In hundreds of county fairs and local festivals, New Yorkers celebrate nature's riches and the joys of harvest season.

The whole village of Marathon turns out in late March or early April to lend a hand at the Central New York Maple Festival. Villagers tap the local maple trees, boil down the sap, and serve up maple sugar candy, sweet maple sundaes, and pancakes with maple syrup.

Farther south, in Owego, the strawberries ripen in June. Music, parades, fireworks, and a lot of pink desserts highlight the Owego Strawberry Festival.

Fall is the time for harvesting apples. New York celebrates its favorite fruit with weekend festivals in dozens of towns and villages. Country clog dancing, old-time fiddling, storytelling, and hayrides are all part of the entertainment. So are baking contests. A few years ago, bakers at the Endicott Apple Fest served up a record-breaking apple strudel that measured one hundred feet long.

With all its industries, western New York still has room for agriculture. Livestock farmers raise hogs, sheep, beef cattle, and dairy cattle. Farmers also grow a variety of crops, including apples, strawberries, cherries, cabbage, sweet corn, snap beans, wheat, oats, and hay. The flat plains near Lake Erie hold cornfields, hayfields, and tangling vines heavy with grapes. Also ideal for grape growing are the gently sloping shores of the Finger Lakes, as well as the Hudson Valley and Long Island. In all these areas, large bodies of water control the temperatures year-round, cooling the summers and warming the winters. Most of the grapes grown in New York are used for juice and wine.

Central and northern New York produce much of America's milk. Many dairy farmers work fields that their grandparents or great-grandparents cleared from forestland. From sunrise to sunset, they feed and milk their herds of dairy cows and tend their fields of silage corn, grown for feed. In some areas overfarming is using up the fertile topsoil. Harry Nye's father and grandfather owned a two-hundred-acre dairy farm in central New York. "Growing up so close to nature gave me an appreciation for the beauty of this region," he said. "In 1959 the farm was declining, mostly due to poor soil. . . . The animals were sold, and the property began the long process of returning to forest."

A young farmer coaxes his dairy cow off a trailer at the Dutchess County Fair Grounds, in the Hudson River valley. More than 1,500 cows, sheep, hogs, and other farm animals are judged for excellence at the annual fair.

In the Adirondacks the soil has always been too thin and rocky for farming. The rocks themselves have often proved valuable. Since the late 1700s, mining companies have extracted minerals such as iron, graphite, talc, sandstone, and granite from the region's abundant deposits. Today many of the mines are closed. However, the region still produces garnet, sometimes called the "Adirondack ruby," which is used in sandpaper and jewelry. The Adirondacks is also the country's only source of high-grade wollastonite. This durable white mineral has a variety of uses, from dental cleaning to car bumpers to match heads.

Trees are another important resource in the Adirondacks. Logging produces hardwoods for furniture, wood pulp for paper, and other forest products.

Mining and logging are both forbidden in much of the Adirondack Park. A patchwork of public and private lands, the park includes more than 6 million acres of forests, streams, and

Garnets are often made into gemstones that are prized for their glittering colors, which can range from brown and green to yellow, pink, and red.

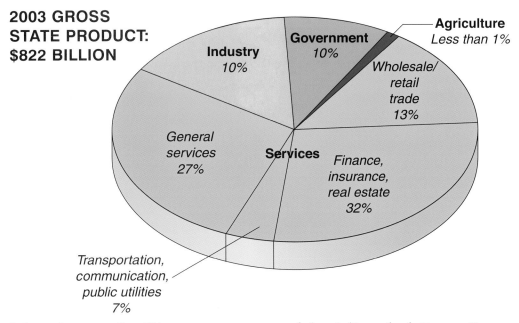

2003 GROSS STATE PRODUCT: $822 BILLION

Industry 10%

Government 10%

Agriculture Less than 1%

Wholesale/retail trade 13%

General services 27%

Services

Finance, insurance, real estate 32%

Transportation, communication, public utilities 7%

lakes. Some 2.6 million acres are part of the Adirondack Forest Preserve, the largest complex of wild public lands in the eastern United States. This wilderness playground is the reason behind the Adirondacks' number-one business, tourism.

Visitors to the Adirondack Forest Preserve can enjoy a variety of recreational activities, including hiking, canoeing, fishing, skiing, and trail rides on mountain bikes and snowmobiles. Jim Bigness of Schenectady is "a regular visitor to the Adirondacks. My sons and I go camping, fishing, and hunting. Let me tell you, there's no better place on earth for roasting the perfect marshmallow and discussing who caught the biggest fish."

Natural and human-made wonders also attract tourists to other parts of the state. In fact, tourism is New York's largest industry. Niagara Falls draws up to 7 million tourists each year, while New York City attracts 40 million visitors from across the country and around the world.

New York also touches the lives of millions of people who will never set foot in the state. Products made in New York are exported to 219 countries. Among the state's leading trading partners are Canada, Japan, the United Kingdom, Switzerland, and Mexico.

In 2000 New York exported $53 billion in goods and services, the third-largest total of any state. Its most important exports included computers and electronic products, transportation equipment, chemicals, and industrial machinery. The production and shipment of exported goods supported the jobs of nearly 310,000 New Yorkers.

Exporters have benefited from free trade agreements between the United States and foreign trading partners. Free trade agreements reduce trade barriers between countries, such as tariffs (import fees), taxes, and

NEW YORK WORKFORCE

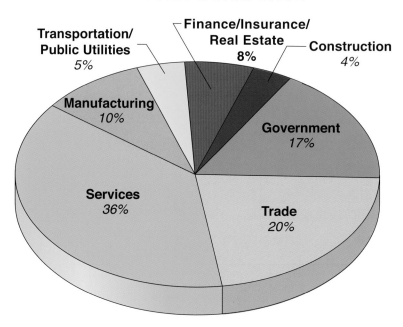

excessive product restrictions. Reducing barriers makes it less expensive for buyers to import goods and easier for sellers to export them.

One trade agreement that has been especially important to New York is the Information Technology Agreement (ITA). By the year 2000, more than sixty nations had signed on as participants. The ITA eliminates tariffs on computers, software, electronic calculators, scientific instruments, and hundreds of other information technology products. It has helped increase exports for New York's many high-tech industries.

While most of the state's trade links

An IBM technician examines a silicon wafer, an essential element in manufacturing microchips for computers and other high-tech products.

with other nations come through the export of products and services, the state is also a leading site for foreign investment. More than three thousand foreign-owned businesses operate in New York, in fields including finance, banking, retail sales, and transportation. Government offices help foreign firms set up and operate throughout the state.

The economy of New York and of the nation are undergoing tremendous changes. In today's global economy, businesses must compete with competitors around the world. Through these challenging times, New York has remained an economic powerhouse, thanks to its rich natural resources, strong government support for business, and the hard work and ingenuity of its people.

Chapter Six

Exploring New York

New York has it all: majestic waterways, unspoiled wilderness, world-class museums, soaring skyscrapers. Let's take a trip around the state and explore some of its many wonders.

THE NORTH COUNTRY

Our journey begins in a leaf-carpeted forest. An hour's hike leads to a view of deep green hills and pools that sparkle like diamonds. Around us stretch nearly six million acres of woods, mountains, lakes, and river valleys. We are in the Adirondack Park, a northern wilderness as big as the state of Vermont.

About half of the Adirondacks is owned by the state and set aside to remain "forever wild." Scattered throughout these unspoiled lands is privately owned property including campgrounds, ski resorts, and more than one hundred villages and small towns. This unusual mix of wilderness and civilization shows New York's commitment to preserving its natural wonders while opening up opportunities to its citizens.

Perched on a rocky outcrop called the Nubble, a hiker looks out over Giant's Washbowl Pond in the Adirondack Mountains.

Celebrating the North Country

North Country New Yorkers are especially proud of their wild, beautiful region. Each August in Massena, in the Saint Lawrence Valley, that pride shines at the Festival of North Country Folklife. The event is dedicated to "slowing down the pace, and appreciating where we came from, if only for a day." Banjo players and fiddlers perform old songs from the logging camps. Craftspeople demonstrate traditional Adirondack crafts such as furniture making, blacksmithing, rug braiding, and woodcarving. The smell of hearty French-Canadian meat pies and pea soup beckons from the food tent. The Talker's Tent serves up another North Country specialty. There old-timers tell outrageous stories about the loggers, hunters, and guides whose adventures are part of the treasury of Adirondack tall tales.

Whiteface Mountain is an example of that commitment. With the highest vertical drop in the East, this popular ski slope is the Adirondacks' only high peak reachable by car (the others must be hiked). In 1935 President Franklin Roosevelt opened the new state highway to the mountaintop. "Many persons cannot indulge in the luxury of camping or climbing," Roosevelt said. "We have now got the means for their coming up here on four wheels."

In the shadow of Whiteface lies Lake Placid, site of the 1932 and 1980 Winter Olympic Games. Young athletes can be seen jogging through this famous lakeside ski town, training for the next Olympics.

Farther north, on Lake Champlain, is Ausable Chasm. Five hundred million years ago, the Ausable River carved this deep path through sandstone. Brave rafters can take a wild ride down the rapids that tumble between the one-hundred-foot cliff walls.

Fort Ticonderoga guards the southern tip of Lake Champlain. Built by the French in 1755, the fort was captured first by the British and then by Patriot forces during the American Revolution. A visit there is like a step back in time. Red-coated soldiers patrol the grounds, parade to the music of fife and drum, and practice firing their Revolutionary-era muskets.

West of the Adirondacks, the Thousand Islands dot the lower Saint Lawrence River. There are actually more than 1,800 islands, some stretching

Fort Ticonderoga guarded American settlements in the Lake Champlain valley during the American Revolution and French and Indian War. Today the restored fortress is a national historic landmark.

more than twenty miles, others measuring just a few feet. One of the most interesting is Heart Island. In 1900 millionaire George Boldt began building a 120-room stone-and-marble castle there for his beloved wife, Louise. Four years later, when Louise suddenly died, all work halted. Today half-finished Boldt Castle is a reminder of fabulous wealth and lost dreams.

WESTERN NEW YORK

From the Thousand Islands, the scenic Seaway Trail leads west along Lake Ontario to the Niagara River. Few wonders can match the awesome sight of the river's drop down a 167-foot rock ledge at Niagara Falls. Seven hundred thousand gallons of water per second cascade over the falls, raising a thunderous roar.

Daredevils have been challenging the falls for more than a century. In 1859 a French tightrope walker known as the Great Blondin walked across on a three-inch-wide rope, carrying his terrified manager on his shoulders. Others have taken the plunge in boats, rubber tubes, and barrels. For those looking for a less dangerous way to explore the area, there are walkways beside the falls, helicopter tours, and boat rides through the mist and spray at the base.

Niagara Falls is western New York's greatest tourist attraction. The thundering waters are also one of the world's greatest sources of hydroelectric power, generating electricity for parts of Canada and northern New York.

PLACES TO SEE

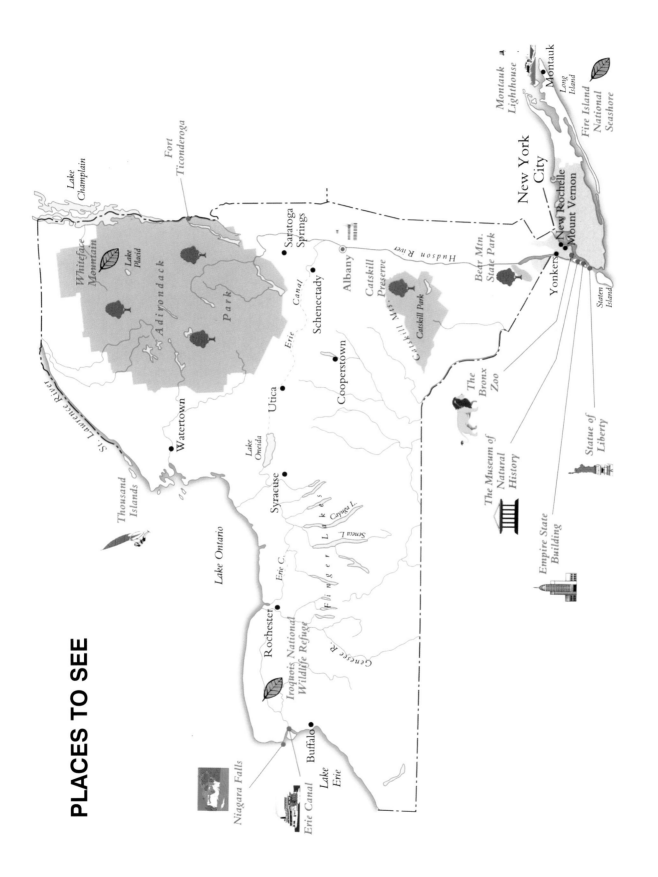

The Finger Lakes region has its own glittering waterfalls, including Taughannock Falls, which is even higher than Niagara. There are also thousands of acres of protected parkland in western New York, plus nature preserves filled with wild plants and animals. Iroquois National Wildlife Refuge is home to hundreds of different types of birds, nesting in marshlands beside Cayuga, Seneca, Onondaga, Oneida, and Mohawk pools. In Letchworth State Park, the Genesee River cuts a seventeen-mile-long canyon through towering rock walls. A statue of a tall woman with long braids marks the grave of Mary Jemison, the "white woman of the Genesee." Captured by a Native American war party at age fifteen, Jemison lived a long, happy life among the Seneca.

The west's big cities and small towns hold many human-made treasures. According to a 2001 survey by the newspaper *USA Today*, Buffalo is the nation's number-one "City with a Heart." Residents love this large city for its small-town feel and its wealth of attractions, including sports stadiums, theaters, fine architecture, and museums.

Rochester has its own impressive museums. The fifty-room mansion of inventor George Eastman houses the International Museum of Photography and Film. There the history of photography unfolds through pictures and hands-on displays.

Located on the eastern shore of Lake Erie, Buffalo has been called the "Queen City of the Great Lakes."

Children explore the history of the American women's movement at the Women's Rights Museum in Seneca Falls.

In Corning glassblowers are often hard at work inside the Museum of Glass. Next door, at the Steuben Factory, skilled craftspeople transform hot liquid glass into delicate crystal.

Seneca Falls was the birthplace of the women's rights movements. Visitors can tour the home of Elizabeth Cady Stanton, who organized America's first women's rights convention in 1848, with the goal of solving "the wrongs of society in general, and of women in particular."

CENTRAL NEW YORK

For a relaxed crossing from western to central New York, travelers can rent a houseboat and cruise the historic Erie Canal. Today New York's canal system is a 524-mile system of waterways that includes not only the 338-mile Erie Canal but also three other canals plus several lakes, reservoirs, and rivers. Boats traveling the full length of the waters wander past nearly two hundred small towns and villages. They must also pass through fifty-seven canal locks. The largest is at Lockport. After a boat floats into the lock's holding chamber, the tenders gently lower it nearly sixty feet to the next water level.

The Erie Canal meets the Hudson River at the state's capital, Albany. A walk through downtown Albany takes in both historic buildings and

Visitors to the Erie Canal take a step back in time, to the days when passengers traveled the waterway on mule-drawn "packet boats."

modern architectural marvels. One of the most impressive sights is the gleaming Empire State Plaza, built by Governor Nelson Rockefeller in the 1960s and 1970s. The plaza's sleek marble-and-glass buildings include a performing arts center, the forty-two-floor Corning Tower, and the New York State Museum. Among the museum's exhibits are a full-size Mohawk longhouse, a hand-carved wooden carousel from the 1890s, and a 1940s New York City subway train. Perhaps the most magnificent building in the plaza is the New York State Capitol. This $25 million granite extravaganza, which took more than thirty years to build, looks like a huge French castle.

Just north of Albany is Saratoga Springs. In the nineteenth century, people flocked there to bathe in the natural mineral springs, which were believed to cure illness. Today horse racing and the arts are this popular resort town's main attractions. A few miles east of town, a winding stairway leads to the top of Saratoga Monument. This 155-foot tower marks the battlefield where Americans claimed their first victory over the British during the Revolutionary War.

Another famous central New York tourist destination is Cooperstown. According to legend, Abner Doubleday invented baseball there in 1839. Cooperstown is the site of the National Baseball Hall of Fame and Museum, dedicated to the game and its players.

THE HUDSON VALLEY

Most travelers heading from Albany to New York City take the fast route, motoring down the New York State Thruway. For a more leisurely journey, boaters can cruise down the Hudson River, past towering cliffs, picture-postcard towns, and million-dollar mansions.

A top attraction along the way is Hyde Park, where the home of President Franklin D. Roosevelt has been left exactly as it was the day he died. Across town is Vanderbilt Mansion. In the Gilded Age, during the late nineteenth century, millionaire Frederick Vanderbilt shipped in craftspeople from Europe to create this spectacular fifty-four-room palace. Farther down the river, the mansion called Boscobel is a masterpiece of the Federal style of architecture, which was popular following the American Revolution. Boscobel was torn down in the 1950s. A group of local residents bought the pieces from the wrecking crew and stored them in their garages until money could be raised to restore the historic mansion.

Across the Hudson from Boscobel is West Point. The U.S. Military Academy at West Point trains young people to become U.S. Army officers. The first fort on this site was built by colonists during the Revolution, on a "point west" of advancing British troops.

Cadets parade on the historic campus of the U.S. Military Academy at West Point, founded in 1778 on the western banks of the Hudson River.

Bear Mountain State Park is the survivor of a different kind of conflict. In the early 1900s, New Yorkers were outraged by a state plan to build a prison on this scenic chunk of shoreline. A group of wealthy businesspeople donated land and large sums of money to turn the area into a park instead. Today millions of visitors come to the park each year to enjoy miles of hiking and cross-country ski trails, lake and river fishing, shaded picnic groves, pools, and playfields.

The lower Hudson Valley is Sleepy Hollow country, made famous by the stories of Washington Irving. Born in New York City five days after the end of the Revolution, Irving went on to become the new nation's first great writer. Many of his most beloved stories, including "The Legend of Sleepy Hollow" and "Rip Van Winkle," were set in New York. Irving's home in Tarrytown, called Sunnyside, is a charming cottage that looks like something straight from the pages of a fairy tale.

A short side trip west leads to the Catskills, the "fairy mountains" where Rip Van Winkle slept for twenty years. The Catskill Mountain region is a paradise of crystal lakes and fresh mountain streams. Catskill Forest Preserve includes 300,000 acres of protected forestland. Fifth grader Dayana Gomez of Monticello, whose family emigrated from the Dominican Republic, loves the Catskills because "the lakes and rivers are so clean and beautiful. There's lots of woods to play in. I like the color of the leaves in fall."

LONG ISLAND

The Hudson River meets the Atlantic Ocean at New York Harbor. Stretching to the east is Long Island.

The north shore of the island has been called the Gold Coast. A string of mansions built by nineteenth-century business tycoons lines its wooded shores. Also found in this area is the five-room log farmhouse where Walt Whitman was born. One of America's most celebrated poets, Whitman spoke of his love for New York City in the poem "Mannahatta": "City of hurried and sparkling waters! city of spires and masts! City nested in bays! my city!"

The bustling village of Sag Harbor, nestled in a bay near the eastern tip of Long Island, was once one of the world's busiest whaling ports. To enter the Sag Harbor Whaling Museum, visitors walk through a giant set of whale's jaws. Inside, exhibits re-create the lives of nineteenth-century whalers.

Montauk Lighthouse stands on Long Island's eastern tip. This sturdy tower was built following the Revolutionary War by order of President George Washington. In those days the lighthouse stood more than two hundred feet from the ocean. Over time, though, crashing waves have worn away the shoreline. Today the lighthouse shines its beacon only about seventy-five feet from the edge of a cliff.

Long Island's southern shore rambles past mile after mile of ocean beaches. Two long sections are parkland, Fire Island National Seashore and Jones Beach State Park.

Montauk Lighthouse has been a part of Long Island's land- and seascape for more than two hundred years, making it the oldest lighthouse in New York State.

On summer days the parks are a perfect place to cool off in the ocean waves that wash the white sand beaches.

NEW YORK CITY

An appropriate end point to a tour of the state is New York City. America's largest city in population, this is one of the most exciting places in the world. The city has everything from zoos, parks, and beaches to museums, theaters, sports stadiums, world-class hotels, restaurants, and shops.

Jazz musicians of the 1930s dubbed New York City the "Big Apple." When they played there, they had finally hit the "big time." The apple is divided into five boroughs: Manhattan, Brooklyn, the Bronx, Queens, and Staten Island. Only the Bronx is part of mainland New York State. The other boroughs are connected to the mainland by bridges and tunnels.

The Brooklyn Bridge, with its spiderweb of steel cables arcing between Brooklyn and Manhattan, is often considered the most beautiful bridge in the world. Coney Island, on Brooklyn's southern tip, is famous for its three-mile beach and amusement park.

When the Brooklyn Bridge was completed in 1883, it was the longest suspension bridge in the world. The web of steel suspension cables and ropes supporting the roadway gave the bridge a remarkable strength and beauty.

Celebrating Brooklyn

Brooklyn is made up of many different neighborhoods, most with a strong ethnic character. Each year people living in all these neighborhoods mingle with ex-Brooklynites returning home for the Welcome Back to Brooklyn festival. This summertime street fair begins with a parade led by the Homecoming King or Queen, a local "graduate" who's gone on to fame. Along the parade route are crafts booths, cultural exhibits, and vendors selling a wide range of international foods. Entertainment is provided by dynamic performers from many cultures. Past stars have included Dairaba West Afrikan Dance Company, Young Soon Kim White Wave Rising Dance Company, and the musical group Roots of Brazil. Festival-goers can also join in street games such as stickball and hopscotch. During the 2000 festival, nearly seven hundred Brooklynites broke the world record for the most people playing marbles at the same time.

The Bronx has high-rise apartments, housing projects, and America's largest city wildlife park, the Bronx Zoo. More than four thousand animals live there in re-creations of their natural habitats, including the indoor Asian rain forest and the Congo Gorilla Forest. The zoo offers visitors a chance to come face-to-face with snow leopards, red pandas, lions, tigers, and bears.

Queens is home to people of so many different nationalities that one subway line has been nicknamed the Multicultural Express. Alongside residential neighborhoods this borough is crowded with office towers, apartments, factories, and two huge airports, LaGuardia International and John F. Kennedy International. Nearly a quarter of Queens is protected parkland. Jamaica Bay Wildlife Refuge has more than nine thousand acres of marshes, fields, woods, ponds, and islands, visited by thousands of birds during their annual migration.

Staten Island is the least populated of the boroughs. Most of the New Yorkers who live there travel by ferryboat to and from jobs in Manhattan. The Staten Island Ferry offers a twenty-five-minute ride with terrific views, all for free!

The smallest borough in size, Manhattan is biggest in just about everything else. American writer Kurt Vonnegut dubbed it "skyscraper national park." Through the years the city has raised a succession of the

TEN LARGEST CITIES

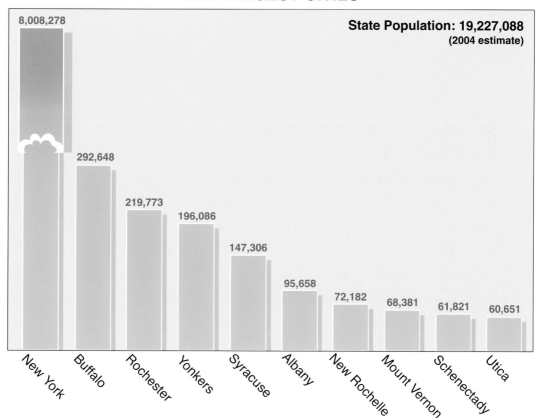

State Population: 19,227,088
(2004 estimate)

City	Population
New York	8,008,278
Buffalo	292,648
Rochester	219,773
Yonkers	196,086
Syracuse	147,306
Albany	95,658
New Rochelle	72,182
Mount Vernon	68,381
Schenectady	61,821
Utica	60,651

Times Square in Manhattan is often called the "crossroads of the world." Lined with stores, restaurants, theaters, and towering office buildings, this bustling district attracts 26 million visitors each year.

tallest buildings in the world, from the Singer, Metropolitan Life, Woolworth, Chrysler, and Empire State buildings to the World Trade Center.

Manhattan has more than 150 museums featuring art, science, music, photography, television, and different ethnic groups and nationalities. The biggest museum is the Metropolitan Museum of Art. The Met's collection of more than two million objects from ancient through modern times includes Egyptian mummies, Joan of Arc's sword and helmet, and an entire living room designed by architect Frank Lloyd Wright. At the American Museum of Natural History, visitors can inspect moon rocks, gigantic dinosaur skeletons, and a ninety-four-foot model of a blue whale.

The World Trade Center Endures

As New Yorkers struggled to recover from the September 11 attacks, one overriding question emerged: what should be done with the World Trade Center site? Some wanted to preserve the sixteen-acre tract of land as a memorial to those who had died. Some called for the construction of new buildings even higher than the Twin Towers. Others envisioned a combination of business space and cultural attractions, bringing new life to this section of downtown Manhattan twenty-four hours a day.

City officials presented their first redevelopment plans in the summer of 2002. A storm of criticism followed. New Yorkers argued that the plans focused too much on business, too little on honoring the September 11 victims. Their protests set in motion a competition among more than four hundred architects and designers worldwide. In early 2003 the World Trade Center design proposal presented by Polish-American architect Daniel Libeskind was selected as the winner.

The centerpiece of Libeskind's inspirational design is a twisting glass-and-steel tower topped by a tall spire. When it is completed, this 1,776-foot Freedom Tower will be the tallest building in the world. Also planned is a permanent memorial called Reflecting Absence, designed by architect Michael Arad. The simple but dramatic memorial will turn the one-acre "footprints" of the Twin Towers into reflecting pools, surrounded by curtains of falling water.

Meanwhile, subway service to the site resumed in late 2003. The rebuilt subway station was christened the World Trade Center station. "It's really a statement of respect for those that died there," said city transportation official Joseph Silverman. "At the same time, I think it's a statement of hope, that the World Trade Center will come back to be a powerful and meaningful development."

An art student perfects his skills by copying a painting by the famous French artist Paul Cézanne at the Metropolitan Museum of Art.

Across town is a floating sea, air, and space museum aboard the World War II aircraft carrier *Intrepid.*

A trip to the city would not be complete without taking in a play. The most famous theaters are on and around Broadway, a wide avenue that runs the entire length of Manhattan. Lincoln Center is a grand complex of buildings devoted to symphony music, opera, and ballet. Radio City Music Hall is America's largest indoor theater. The famous Radio City Rockettes, a line of long-legged dancers, perform their famous precision steps and kicks at the start of each movie or stage show.

Radio City is just one of nineteen buildings in an eleven-acre business and entertainment complex called Rockefeller Center. Built by millionaire John D. Rockefeller, Jr., in the 1930s, the center is like a city within a city. It contains office buildings, shops, restaurants, movie theaters, and a sunken plaza with an outdoor skating rink. Towering overhead is a golden statue of a famous figure from Greek mythology, Prometheus.

To see a nation within a city, visitors can head to the United Nations Headquarters. This building is considered international territory, so those who enter have officially left the United States. Headphones in the Visitors' Gallery allow curious onlookers to listen as representatives from 191 member states discuss how to work together peacefully.

One of the world's greatest symbols of freedom and peace between nations stands in New York Harbor. The Statue of Liberty was a gift from

France to the United States. Sculptor Frédéric Auguste Bartholdi shipped the pieces to America in 214 crates. In 1886 the 152-foot copper statue was placed on a pedestal on Liberty Island. For boatloads of European immigrants, the sight of the gleaming lady with the blazing torch meant the end of a long journey toward hope and freedom.

Today the Statue of Liberty is a national monument. A museum at its base honors the struggles and contributions of America's immigrants. Those who climb the spiral staircase to the statue's observation deck are rewarded with a sweeping view across the harbor, to the city those immigrants led to greatness. It is a good place to end our journey, where so many Americans began theirs—at New York Harbor, jewel of the state that is the crown of the nation.

In the course of nearly six decades, the Statue of Liberty in New York Harbor welcomed millions of seafaring immigrants to America's shores.

THE FLAG: The flag was officially adopted in 1909. It shows the state seal on a dark blue background. New York's seal was first painted on a silk flag for the Third New York Regiment during the American Revolution.

THE SEAL: Adopted in 1882, the seal shows two women holding a shield. The blindfolded woman represents Justice; the other stands for Liberty. Within the shield are two Hudson River ships with a sun rising over a mountain. The shield is topped by a bald eagle with outstretched wings. The ribbon beneath the women's feet displays the state motto in Latin, Excelsior.

State Survey

Statehood: July 26, 1788

Origin of Name: Named to honor England's Duke of York and Albany, who later became King James II

Nickname: The Empire State

Capital: Albany

Motto: Ever Upward

Bird: Bluebird

Animal: Beaver

Fish: Brook trout

Flower: Rose

Tree: Sugar maple

Gem: Garnet

Fruit: Apple

Beverage: Milk

Muffin: Apple muffin

Bluebird

Rose

THE NEW COLOSSUS

Although many songs have been written in praise of New York, the state has, in fact, no official song. There is one symbol that speaks to all New Yorkers and all other Americans as well: the Statue of Liberty. Emma Lazarus wrote the poem, "The New Colossus," which is inscribed on a tablet at the base of the statue. Jerry Silverman has put her words to music.

Words by Emma Lazarus
Music by Jerry Silverman
(Used by permission)

Highest Point: Mount Marcy in the Adirondack Mountains—5,344 feet

Lowest Point: Sea level along the Atlantic coast

Area: 49,108 square miles

Greatest Distance, North to South: 310 miles

Greatest Distance, East to West (including Long Island): 450 miles

Bordering States: Vermont, Massachusetts, and Connecticut to the east, New Jersey and Pennsylvania to the south, a piece of Pennsylvania to the west

Hottest Recorded Temperature: 108°F at Troy on July 22, 1926

Coldest Recorded Temperature: -52°F at Old Forge on February 18, 1979

Average Annual Precipitation: 39 inches

Major Rivers: Hudson, Mohawk, Saint Lawrence, Delaware, Black, Genessee, Niagara, Oswego, Susquehanna, Saranac, Ausable

Major Lakes: Erie, Ontario, Champlain, George, Oneida, Seneca, Cayuga, Sacandaga, Canandaigua, Chautauqua, Black, Saranac, Placid

Trees: sugar maple, birch, aspen, oak, elm, hickory, beech, white pine, shortleaf pine, spruce, fir, red cedar, ash, hemlock, laurel, sweet gum, cherry

Wild Plants: rose, bleeding heart, Jacob's ladder, violet, Indian pipes, Queen Anne's lace, buttercup, daisy, black-eyed Susan, goldenrod, devil's paintbrush, toothwort, bittersweet, dandelion, clover, trillium

Bleeding heart

Animals: beaver, white-tailed deer, black bear, wildcat, red fox, muskrat, raccoon, skunk, rabbit, chipmunk, squirrel, porcupine, woodchuck, shrew, opossum, wood frog, garden snake, eastern rattlesnake, copperhead

Birds: bluebird, blue jay, cardinal, sparrow, robin, meadowlark, swallow, thrush, chickadee, woodpecker, wren, crow, oriole, plover, rock dove, mourning dove, barn owl, loon, Canada goose, pheasant, partridge, wild duck, wild turkey, bald eagle, peregrine falcon, hawk, gull, tern

Fish: lake trout, rainbow trout, pickerel, pike, perch, sunfish, crappie, bass, salmon, bullhead, flounder, fluke, tuna, blackfish, weakfish, bluefish, striped bass, swordfish, shad, squid, mussels, lobster

Endangered Animals: Indiana bat, gray wolf, cougar, sperm whale, right whale, finback whale, eastern woodrat, peregrine falcon, piping plover, bog turtle, leatherback turtle, hawksbill sea turtle, round whitefish, shortnose sturgeon, pugnose shiner, deepwater sculpin, karner blue butterfly, dwarf wedge mussel

Endangered Plants: bleeding heart, alpine azalea, small white ladyslipper, Jacob's ladder, Houghton's goldenrod, coastal violet, silvery aster, Michigan lily, mountain watercress, dwarf white birch, dwarf willow, willow oak, Virginia pine

TIME LINE

New York History

1524 Giovanni Verrazano enters New York Harbor

c. 1570 Iroquois League established

1609 Henry Hudson sails up the Hudson River, later named for him

1609 Samuel de Champlain explores around Lake Champlain

1624 Dutch establish settlement at Fort Orange (now Albany)

1664 English take over New Netherland and rename it New York

1734 John Peter Zenger acquitted of libel, laying the foundation for freedom of the press

1754 Albany Congress attempts to unite the colonies

1765 Stamp Act Congress meets in Albany

1775 American Revolution begins; Americans capture Fort Ticonderoga

1776 British capture New York City

1777 Americans win the Battle of Saratoga

1783 American Revolution ends

1785 New York City becomes the nation's capital for five years

1788 New York becomes the eleventh state

1802 West Point Military Academy opens

1807 Steamship *Clermont* sails up the Hudson from New York City to Albany

1814 British defeated at the Battle of Plattsburg during the War of 1812

1825 The Erie Canal opens, linking the Hudson River to Lake Erie

1827 Slavery is abolished in the state

1831 Mohawk & Hudson Railroad opens

1848 First women's rights convention held in Seneca Falls

1861–1865 The Civil War

1863 New Yorkers riot over Civil War draft laws

1883 The Brooklyn Bridge is completed

1886 The Statue of Liberty is dedicated

1898 Brooklyn, Manhattan, the Bronx, Queens, and Staten Island are united to form Greater New York City

1909 The National Association for the Advancement of Colored People (NAACP) is founded in New York City

1911 Fire at the Triangle Shirtwaist Factory kills 146 people and leads to labor reform

1928 New York Barge Canal System opens

1929 Stock market crashes in New York City; Great Depression begins

1931 Empire State Building is completed in New York City

1939 New York World's Fair opens in Flushing Meadows in Queens

1946 New York City is chosen as the site of the United Nations

1959 The Saint Lawrence Seaway opens

1964 The Verrazano-Narrows Bridge, the world's longest suspension bridge, opens

1980 Lake Placid hosts the Winter Olympic Games

1989 David Dinkins is elected New York City's first black mayor

1993 Ruth Bader Ginsburg of Brooklyn is second woman nominated to the U.S. Supreme Court

2001 Terrorists attack the World Trade Center, killing nearly 2,800

2004 The cornerstone is laid for the Freedom Tower at the World Trade Center site

ECONOMY

Natural Resources: fish and shellfish, lumber, granite, sand, emery, gypsum, salt, natural gas, oil, limestone, zinc, garnet

Agricultural Products: dairy and beef cattle, pigs, sheep, chickens, ducks, eggs, apples, cherries, grapes, carrots, celery, onions, cabbage, beets, potatoes, corn, honey, maple syrup

Manufacturing: printing materials, scientific instruments, machinery, chemicals, optical equipment, photographic materials, computers, paper, processed food, textiles, glass

Dairy cows

Business and Trade: wholesale and retail trade, banking, finance, communications, publishing, advertising, entertainment, tourism

STATE STARS

Bella Abzug (1920–1998), born in New York City, became a leading figure in the women's liberation movement of the 1960s. As a representative in Congress, she fought hard to see that the city got its fair share of federal money. She once suggested that New York City might become a state. In 1995 Abzug led a group to the women's conference in Beijing, China.

Susan B. Anthony (1820–1906) was one of the foremost leaders of women's struggle for the right to vote. From her home in Rochester, Anthony planned, wrote, and campaigned. Her constant message was "Failure is impossible."

Mariah Carey (1970–   ), from Huntington, began writing songs as a teenager and knew she wanted to be a singer. In New York City, she got her big break and began recording. Her first album, *Mariah Carey,* sold six million copies and won two Grammys. Later albums also sold in the millions.

Shirley Chisholm

Shirley Chisholm (1924–   ), born in Brooklyn, was the first black woman to be elected to Congress. In 1972 she became the first African American to run for president as a Democrat. Chisholm went on to become a lecturer and speaker.

Grover Cleveland (1837–1908) of Buffalo served as mayor of that city, governor of New York, and in 1884 was elected president of the United States. Known for his honesty, Cleveland opposed the bosses who ran the political machines of the day and fought vigorously against corruption.

Peter Cooper (1791–1883) of New York City designed and built the "Tom Thumb," the first steam locomotive in the United States. With his own money, Cooper founded Cooper Union for the Advancement of Science and Art in New York City's East Village, a tuition-free school for engineers and artists.

Peter Cooper

Mario Cuomo (1932–   ) was born in Queens, the son of immigrant parents from Italy. He practiced law and then entered public service. Cuomo served as New York's secretary of state, lieutenant governor, and in 1982 was elected the state's fifty-second governor. As governor, Cuomo championed the rights of women, minorities, and the disabled and worked for social and political reform. Known as a dynamic speaker, he delivered many eloquent speeches during his twelve years in office.

Joseph (Joe) DiMaggio (1914–1999) was born in California but rose to fame in New York. "The Yankee Clipper" played center field for the New York Yankees for thirteen seasons. Voted the American League's most valuable player in 1939, 1941, and 1947, DiMaggio was elected to the Baseball Hall of Fame in 1955.

George Eastman (1854–1932) was a pioneer in film and photography. Born in Waterville, Eastman was a high-school dropout who became a clerk in a bank in Rochester. Working at night, Eastman devised a way to put film on a roll. In 1888 he came out with the first Kodak camera. Four years later, he founded the Eastman Kodak Company.

Julius Erving (1950–   ), known as "Dr. J," grew up in Roosevelt, Long Island. Playing basketball for the New York Nets in the 1970s, he invented the "over the rim" technique with his spectacular leaping ability.

George Gershwin (1898–1937) grew up in New York City listening to all kinds of music. As a composer, he blended different musical styles to create, often with his brother Ira as a collaborator, such works as *Rhapsody in Blue,* the musical *Lady Be Good,* and the famous folk opera *Porgy and Bess.*

Mel Gibson (1956–   ) may have an Australian accent, but he was born in Peekskill. Moving to Australia as a boy, Gibson made his mark in the Australian science fiction films *Mad Max* and *Road Warrior*. He went to Hollywood, where he became well known as an actor in movies including *Lethal Weapon* and as the director of the 2004 blockbuster *The Passion of the Christ.*

Ruth Bader Ginsburg (1933–), from Brooklyn, graduated first in her class at Harvard. She was the first permanent female law professor at Columbia University and the founder of the Women's Rights Project. Bader Ginsburg also served as a federal judge. In 1993 she became the second woman appointed to the U.S. Supreme Court.

Ruth Bader Ginsburg

Alexander Hamilton (1755–1804) was born in the West Indies and came to New York City to attend Columbia University. After serving in the American Revolution, Hamilton was appointed secretary of the treasury in the new U.S. government. He laid the foundation for the economic policy of the young United States. Hamilton believed that industry would make the nation strong. He fought for the adoption of the U.S. Constitution and founded the *New York Post,* a newspaper still published today. He was killed in a duel by Aaron Burr.

Langston Hughes (1902–1967) was born in Joplin, Missouri. Moving to New York City, he became famous as a major poet of the Harlem Renaissance of the 1920s. Much of his work expressed the struggle of African Americans. Hughes also wrote several children's books, including *The Sweet and Sour Animal Book* and *The Dream Keeper.*

Fiorello LaGuardia (1882–1947) was born in New York City. Nicknamed the "Little Flower," he won the hearts of New Yorkers through his honesty and reform programs. As mayor from 1934 to 1945, LaGuardia supported urban renewal, the rights of workers, and housing and health programs for the poor. A colorful person, he read the comics to children over the radio during a newspaper strike. Once, as a mediator during a coal strike in the city, he turned off the heat in a meeting room when the two sides could not agree.

Emma Lazarus (1849–1887) was born in New York City. Well known as a poet, Lazarus also became involved in the cause of Jewish immigrants who were fleeing Russian tyranny in the 1880s. When she was asked to write a verse for the base of the Statue of Liberty, she composed the now-famous poem "The New Colossus."

Barbara McClintock (1902–1992), raised in Brooklyn, spent her career studying genetics. At her laboratory in Cold Spring Harbor, while doing research on corn, she found that genes can "jump" from one chromosome to another. This was a groundbreaking explanation of hereditary patterns. For her discovery, McClintock received the Nobel Prize for Physiology in 1983.

Anna Mary Robertson Moses (1860–1961), known as Grandma Moses, was born in Washington County. For most of her life, she ran her own farm. Moses once said that she probably would have raised chickens if she hadn't become a painter. Starting in her seventies, she began turning out canvases of "old-timey" farm life from her home in Eagle Bridge. Among her one thousand paintings are *The Old Checkered House, Black Horses,* and *Hoosick Valley (From the Window).*

Joseph Pulitzer (1847–1911), an immigrant from Hungary, became New York City's leading newspaper publisher in the late 1800s. Through his paper, the *New York World,* Pulitzer fought political corruption and crusaded for reform. By 1887 the *World* had the largest circulation of any paper in the nation. Pulitzer went on to found Columbia University's School of Journalism and established the Pulitzer Prizes for achievements in journalism, literature, drama, and music.

Geraldo Rivera (1943–   ), journalist and TV talk show host, was born in New York City. As a television news reporter, he exposed the terrible conditions in a home for the mentally disabled in 1972. He later became a TV talk show host with his program *Geraldo.*

Diann Roffe-Steinrotter (1968–   ) began skiing at the age of two near her home in Rochester. In 1985 she won her first World Cup event, the giant slalom at Lake Placid. She won an Olympic silver medal for the giant slalom in 1992 but kept her sights on winning a gold. In 1994 she triumphed over a bad starting position to win the Women's Super Giant Slalom and her gold medal.

Eleanor Roosevelt

Eleanor Roosevelt (1884–1962) was born in New York City. She married Franklin Roosevelt in 1905 and went on to become one of the most active of the nation's first ladies. A humanitarian and reformer, she became known as the First Lady of the World. She wrote her own newspaper column, advised her husband on many social and political issues, and was a strong champion of African-American rights.

Franklin Roosevelt (1882–1945) was born in Hyde Park to a well-to-do New York family. As the thirty-second president, he led the nation during the Great Depression of the 1930s and through World War II. His New Deal programs included social relief and reform and more federal control over business and industry. His radio "Fireside Chats" let Americans know that their government was working to help them.

Jonas Salk (1914–1995), born in New York City, began his research on the polio virus at the University of Pittsburgh, where he developed a vaccine for polio. The first tests on children began in 1952, and by 1955 the vaccine had become available for the general public. Dr. Salk spent his final years working on a vaccine for AIDS.

Beverly Sills (1929–   ) was born Belle Silverman in New York City. She began performing on the radio at age four and went on to become a major opera soprano and recording star. A dynamic and creative manager, she took over the failing New York City Opera in 1979 and greatly improved its finances and its image.

Jonas Salk

Denzel Washington

Denzel Washington (1954–   ), born in Mount Vernon, first became well known playing the role of a doctor in the television series *St. Elsewhere*. In 1989 he won an Oscar as Best Supporting Actor in the film *Glory*. He won the Oscar for Best Actor in 2002 for his performance in *Training Day*.

Edith Wharton (1862–1937), a native of New York City, wrote about the lives and manners of turn-of-the-century upper-class New York society. One of her best-known novels, *The Age of Innocence,* won the 1921 Pulitzer Prize for Fiction and was made into a successful motion picture in 1993.

Vanessa Williams (1963–), raised in Millwood, was the first African-American Miss America. Her musical talent has helped her achieve stardom. Williams's first album, *The Right Stuff,* went gold in 1988, and her second album, *Comfort Zone,* went platinum. In 1994 she starred in the Broadway show *Kiss of the Spider Woman.*

CALENDAR OF CELEBRATIONS

Saranac Lake celebrates snow and ice in February with the nation's oldest winter carnival. Visitors watch hockey tournaments, skating races, and torchlight skiing. The festival ends with a fireworks display called "storming the ice palace."

New York City's Irish heritage is celebrated in March with the Saint Patrick's Day Parade. The Grand Marshal leads bagpipers, fife and drum corps, and bands from city departments up Fifth Avenue. Scores of bands from schools and communities around the nation join them. New York politicians often put in an appearance at this parade.

Jamestown honors its famous daughter Lucille Ball with an annual Lucyfest. The May celebration includes films as well as live comedy performances that are a good showcase for new comedians. Visitors can tour various "Lucy" sites and go to an auction of Lucy mementos.

Saint Patrick's Day Parade in New York City

Tulips, which came to New York with the early Dutch settlers, are the special feature of Albany's yearly Tulip Festival in May. Festival-goers enjoy some 50,000 blooming tulips, along with music, exhibits, and a bicycle race through the city. A Tulip Queen is crowned at the end of the celebration.

New York City's International Food Festival stretches for twenty blocks along Ninth Avenue each May. Often called the city's biggest block party, it is also the oldest. Some three hundred different foods from about thirty cultures remind New Yorkers of their rich ethnic heritage.

A yellow brick road runs down the center of Chittenango, honoring the town's native son L. Frank Baum, the author of *The Wonderful Wizard of Oz*. An annual May Ozfest features an Ozparade and an Ozcraft show.

Old Forge has a unique way to celebrate Father's Day in June. The townspeople hold a frog-jumping contest. From large to small, from fat to thin, frogs leap around on the town's tennis court. There is also an "ugly tie" contest for dads.

Cape Vincent residents celebrate their North Country French-Canadian heritage in July with a French Festival. Artisans create traditional crafts, and there is plenty of authentic French food and pastries. Fireworks and a parade top off the festival.

Cobleskill is the home of the yearly Iroquois Indian Festival. On Labor Day weekend, Iroquois men and women gather to celebrate their heritage. They perform special ceremonies and dances, play traditional games, and serve authentic foods. Iroquois crafts are also on display.

A "run for the pasta" is a feature of Watertown's Bravo Italiano Festival in September. Men and women dress in traditional Italian costumes and celebrate their heritage with food, music, and games. One special game is bocce, an old Italian bowling game.

Paying tribute to the apple is a favorite New York pastime. At Lockport's Apple Country Festival in October, visitors can view the world's largest cider barrel and feast on apple pancakes.

The Harvest Festival at Wappingers Falls in October celebrates the Hudson Valley's early settlers and the valley's environment. Folk songs, banjo bands, and a dance called clogging are featured, along with wildlife talks and farm demonstrations.

Visitors and residents start early to find good spots to view Macy's Thanksgiving Day Parade in New York City. Santa Claus rides by while gigantic balloons depicting famous cartoon characters float overhead. The night before, many people gather to watch as the balloons are inflated near Central Park.

TOUR THE STATE

Fort Ontario (Oswego). Military drills and exhibits trace the history of this fortress, which was used as a training center and garrison for soldiers from the French and Indian War through World War II.

John Brown State Historic Site (North Elba) is the nineteenth-century farm and burial place of the famous abolitionist.

Lake Placid Winter Olympic Training Center (Lake Placid). In addition to holding all kinds of winter sports events, Lake Placid is the site of the Olympic Training Center, a training ground for athletes from around the world.

Ausable Chasm (Ausable). This famous gorge was carved out by the Ausable River on its way to Lake Champlain. Visitors can take an exciting boat ride through the river's swift rapids.

Fort Crailo Museum (Rensselaer) re-creates early Dutch life in the Hudson Valley with furniture, household items, and a working kitchen.

National Baseball Hall of Fame and Museum (Cooperstown) honors those who have excelled in playing and managing baseball and houses exhibits tracing the history of the game.

Saratoga National Historic Park (Stillwater). Programs and activities commemorate the two Revolutionary battles that took place on this vast battlefield.

United States Military Academy at West Point conducts parades and reviews for visitors. Its military museum is the largest in the world. Visitors can also see links from a chain that was stretched across the Hudson River to block British ships during the American Revolution.

Sunnyside (Tarrytown) was the home of author Washington Irving, who is most well known for his two tales about early Dutch settlers, "Rip Van Winkle" and "The Legend of Sleepy Hollow." Irving added gables, fancy chimneys, and a tall tower to the original Dutch farmer's house to create this fairy-tale cottage.

Franklin D. Roosevelt National Historic Site (Hyde Park) contains the home of America's thirty-second president. Also on the site is the Presidential Library and Museum, containing many of Roosevelt's books, papers, and personal belongings as well as the papers of Eleanor Roosevelt.

Statue of Liberty National Monument (Liberty Island, New York City). Exhibits at the base of the statue tell the story of immigration from 1600 to the present. Visitors can look inside the statue through a glass ceiling and climb to the observation deck for views of New York City and New York Harbor.

Ellis Island National Monument (New York City). Restored buildings and exhibits of immigrant artifacts commemorate the thousands of people who passed through the doors of Ellis Island to enter America.

Brooklyn Children's Museum (New York City). Hands-on exhibits let young visitors jump up and down on giant piano keys to make music or try out beds from different countries. In the Animal Diner, children can push buttons to make animals light up, showing the kinds of foods they eat.

Bronx Zoo (New York City) is the largest city zoo in the country. Nearly four thousand animals of some 450 different species live in specially arranged open areas re-creating their natural habitat.

Ganondagan "Town of Peace" Historic Site (Victor). Ganondagan is the state's only Native American historic site. It is located where a seventeenth-century Seneca village once stood. Signs along ancient foot trails tell the story of the Seneca people.

Corning Glass Center (Corning) has a factory that makes special art glass. Its library has thousands of books on glassmaking, and a museum contains exhibits covering 3,500 years of glassmaking.

Niagara Falls (Niagara Falls). Visitors can marvel at one of the world's natural wonders while taking a boat ride to the foot of Niagara Falls or walking down a winding staircase to the base of the falls.

George Eastman House (Rochester) is filled with collections about photography, the technology of film, and camera exhibits. There are nature walks in the gardens. A discovery room encourages hands-on activities.

Women's Rights National Historic Park (Seneca Falls) includes the restored home of Elizabeth Cady Stanton, an early leader in the women's rights movement.

Samuel Wilson of Troy is said to have been the model for the character Uncle Sam. Wilson was a meat packer who sold supplies to the U.S. Army during the War of 1812. He stamped his barrels of meat with the initials U.S. When asked what the initials stood for, someone responded, "Uncle Sam Wilson." That led to the idea of Uncle Sam as a symbol for the U.S. government. Cartoonists later gave the character his modern image, with a white beard, tall hat, and star-spangled suit.

Some sources say that New York State got its nickname, the "Empire State," from George Washington. In 1784 Washington told New York's first governor, George Clinton, that the state was "at present the Seat of the Empire."

Find Out More

BOOKS

Bial, Raymond. *The Iroquois.* Lifeways series. New York: Marshall Cavendish, 1999.

Elish, Dan. *New York.* It's My State series. New York: Marshall Cavendish, 2003.

Gelman, Amy. *New York.* Hello USA series. Minneapolis: Lerner, 2002.

Maynard, Christopher. *Kids' New York.* New York: Dorling Kindersley, 2000.

Naden, Corinne J., and Rose Blue. *New York: A MyReportLinks.com Book.* Berkeley Heights, NJ: Enslow, 2002.

Stewart, Mark. *New York: Native Peoples.* Chicago: Heinemann Library, 2003.

————. *New York: Plants and Animals.* Chicago: Heinemann Library, 2003.

————. *People of New York.* Chicago: Heinemann Library, 2003.

Sturm, Ellen. *New York.* Land of Liberty series. Mankato, MN: Capstone Press, 2003.

Wheeler, Jill C. *September 11, 2001: The Day That Changed America.* Edina, MN: Abdo Publishing, 2002.

Witheridge, Annette. *New York Then and Now.* San Diego, CA: Thunder Bay Press, 2000.

VIDEOTAPES

New York: A Documentary Film, Warner Home Video, 2003. (Eight-volume video set based on a PBS series explores the history of New York from Dutch settlement in the early 1800s through the World Trade Center attacks on September 11, 2001.)

New York City, MPI Home Video, 1999. 58 minutes. (Native New Yorkers introduce visitors to sites not usually seen by tourists.)

WEB SITES

Ellis. Copyright The Statue of Liberty-Ellis Island Foundation, Inc., 2000
http://www.ellisisland.org
Click on "Immigrant Experience" for a time line of immigration and stories of Americans from different backgrounds who have researched their ancestry.

Empire State Building Official Internet Site. http://www.esbnyc.com
Click on "ESB Virtual Tour" for a photographic tour of the Empire State Building. The site also includes artwork submitted by young visitors to the famous skyscraper.

Get the Facts about New York State. New York State Department of
State. http://www.dos.state.ny.us/kidsroom/nysfacts/factmenu.html
Check out this site for fast facts on New York history, government,
state symbols, and more.

I Love New York: New York State for Kids. Copyright New York State
Department of Economic Development, 2002.
http://www.iloveny.com/kids/index.asp
This site offers "kid-friendly" information on travel, recreation,
attractions, and upcoming events throughout the state, as well as puzzles, games, and postcards.

Learning Adventures in Citizenship: From New York to Your Town.
www.pbs.org/wnet/newyork/laic
At this companion to the PBS series *New York: A Documentary Film,*
you can explore the history of New York and find activities for
exploring the history of your own town.

New York Kids. Copyright WNYC, 1999. http://www.nykids.org
This companion site to the "New York Kids" radio program, broad-
cast by WNYC, offers music, jokes, games, puzzles, and more, all
designed to help you learn about New York City.

New York State. www.state.ny.us
New York State's official Web site offers information on government,
law, education, the environment, and much more. There are also
news articles, maps, and links to state agencies providing a variety of
information and services.

100 Years of New York City. Copyright The New York Times Company, 1998. http://www.nytimes.com/specials/nyc100

Articles and photos from *The New York Times* archives offer a decade-by-decade glimpse into the past one hundred years of New York City history.

ABOUT THE AUTHOR

Virginia Schomp has written more than fifty titles for young readers on topics including dolphins, dinosaurs, occupations, American history, and world history. With her husband, Richard, and their son, Chip, she makes her home in Monticello, in the heart of New York's Catskill Mountains.

Index

Page numbers in boldface are illustrations and charts.